"I feel privileged Anastacia's life. The story drew me in so tightly I felt loss after the book finished. Anastacia exhibits a transparency in sharing her lessons that allows her readers to feel their own vulnerability. It is truly an honor to be touched and lifted by Anastacia's raw heart." – Linda Curry, author of *Pebbles of Gold* and founder of True Balance Wellness.

"This journey from powerlessness into self-awareness, self-transformation and freedom is one of the most powerful I have ever read. Its writing is brilliant and its spiritual power is profound. I've shared its story with more than 200 people, and they were all deeply inspired – as was I." ~David McArthur, author of *Your Spiritual Heart*.

"First, I have to say WOW!!
It was a beautiful story. I felt like I was in each moment, right there with you. Your words are so powerful. While I was reading it, there were moments when I took a breath and thought, "She is just like me." I see now that you have indeed taken your power back. I will use it as a way to help others. We all get Shattered Into Being; that is how we release our inner light. The ending made me feel strong and hopeful. It helped me think of my own life, and how I too have been a Beacon Shattered Into Being. Thank you for such an amazing book, and for sharing it with me. I look forward to reading more of your books and blogs." ~Yvonne Williams, author of *A Drop of Water*.

"I just finished reading your book. It is a very compelling read, and well written. I think it is a story of survival, and just as the book you were given at the women's shelter did for you, it will help others to know that they are not alone. I think it is important in this way – and a gift." ~JMS

Dedication

To every being and all the storms that have helped me on my journey, following the North Star, the light, within my heart. Through it all I have remembered the Source of all healing, the power to transform suffering into light, in service of all sentient beings. I have remembered the power of Love.

To my adversaries, supporters and guardians who have helped me remember who I am. They have shaped my character, developed my self-esteem and deepened my confidence and belief in myself. Without these relationships I could never have become empowered as the survivor that I am today.

Copyright @ 2016 Anastacia Jayet

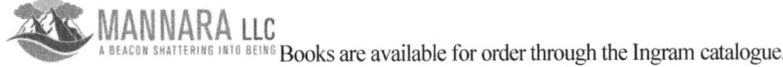 Books are available for order through the Ingram catalogue.

All rights reserved. No part of this book may be reproduced or utilized in any form or by any means, electronic process, phonographic recording, mechanical, including photocopying, recording, or by any information storage and retrieval system, transmitted, or otherwise copied for public or private use – other than "fair use" as brief quotations embodied in articles and reviews – without prior written permission from the author. A credit must appear, with Title and Author, for press, write-ups, articles or reviews using excerpts from **Shattered Into Being; A Beacon Shattering Into Being, by Anastacia Jayet**, AnastaciaJayet.com

Cover and Graphic Design By: Lulu Cuarteros

Disclaimer

This is my story – my truth as I have experienced it, perceived it and believed it to be at the time. I do not pretend to know the motivations, perceptions or intentions of others. My experience is mine alone. My perception of the actions of others has been colored by my own beliefs, values and expressions. This is how I experienced the words, actions and intentions of others through my own filters of limitation and belief. There is no intention to judge, malign or cause harm to any character represented in this book, both living or dead. All names in this book have been changed to protect the anonymity of those concerned. The author is held harmless and assumes no responsibility for any attempt by any outside party to contact, discover or investigate the true identity of any character represented. The author of this book does not dispense medical advice or prescribe the use of any technique as a form of treatment for physical, emotional, or medical problems without the advice of a physician, either directly or indirectly. The intent of the author is to offer information of a general nature to help you in your quest for emotional and/or spiritual well-being. In the event you use any information in this book for yourself, which is your constitutional right, the author and the publisher assume no responsibility for your actions.

For more information on future works, events and blogs, visit AnastaciaJayet.com

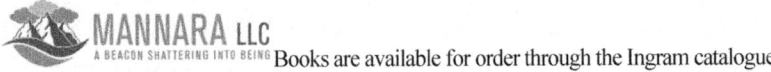 Books are available for order through the Ingram catalogue.

Printed in the United States of America
First Printing: August 2016
Published by Sojourn Publishing, LLC

ISBN: 978-1-62747-038-4
eBook ISBN: 978-1-62747-020-9

Shattered Into Being

A BEACON SHATTERING INTO BEING

By Anastacia Jayet

Acknowledgments

In heartfelt gratitude and appreciation, I thank my husband and three children. They have shown me unlimited support and patience as I wrote this book. I acknowledge the deep trust my husband has placed in me, as I reveal our most intimate secrets of struggle and devoted love. He has been my knight in shining armor, even when I struggled to believe in his love or his desire to protect me at all costs.

I acknowledge that I have received guidance, support and love from both the seen and the unseen worlds. At exactly the right moment in time, all of my needs have been met, all my desires realized – without exception. I have never been alone, not even in my darkest hours. I have been held in love for all eternity, through all time and all space, and in every dimension.

I acknowledge the critical role that nature has played in my life. I have run to her, hidden in her trees, climbed her mountains and played in her forests all my life. I have absorbed her rays of sunlight through my entire being, felt her winds of change penetrate my awareness and witnessed the majesty and beauty of her storms. I have found solace, companionship and the healing power of love by becoming one with nature. I could not have survived this journey through life without her.

I want to say a special thanks to fellow authors David McArthur of *Your Spiritual Heart*, Yvonne Williams of *A Drop of Water* and Linda Curry of *Pebbles of Gold,* who shared their stories with me. In sharing, I learned to understand my own story so much more. They have encouraged, supported and uplifted me when I needed it most. Please consider reading their inspiring works.

I also want to give a heartfelt thank you to Tom Bird and his talented team at Sojourn Publishing, LLC, including Sabrina Fritts, Executive Director; Mary Stevenson, personal assistant to Tom Bird; Idony Lisle, style editor; Rosina Wilson, copyeditor and Denise Cassino, book-marketing specialist.

To my friend Adrienne DeGuerre who agreed to read my book and give me her gut intuition at a moment's notice, without complaint or hesitation – the day before her birthday, no less!

I have changed all the names in this book to protect the privacy of those concerned. Not everyone is as comfortable with the raw and honest truth of their experiences in life as I am.

Prologue

This is my story, my truth as I have experienced it, perceived it and believed it to be at the time. I do not pretend to know the motivations or perceptions of others. My experience is mine alone. My perception of the actions of others has been colored by my own beliefs, values and expressions. This is how I experienced the words, actions and intentions of others through my own filters of limitation and belief.

It is my intention that others know they are not alone, and that their journeys and stories are important. The more we share our stories, the greater healing we can experience – releasing, forgiving and allowing ourselves to be loved once more. In sharing we learn, we become vulnerable and we are forced to face ourselves. This is how we find our way back to the power within. It is how we find the healing power of love, and the gentle guidance of the still small voice within our hearts. This voice speaks to us as we learn our pattern – the singular lesson of this life – expressed in a thousand ways. This is the kernel of truth, the seed, that has matured as we journey through life.

Once we know the nature of our seed, our pattern, we are empowered. We are transformed from victim to creator through compassion, forgiveness and understanding. The storms of life are as much a blessing as are the gifts along the way. Gratitude, humility and integrity guide us on the path to wisdom. A pure heart will reveal the truth within; the unlimited power of love to heal and transform all suffering into light.

We are afforded the opportunity to choose to help others find their own truth, as we continue to share our stories, patterns and struggles to live life on purpose. It is always a choice to share what a life filled with value and meaning can be. Living life in service to all sentient beings is the expression of transformation in form.

Contents

Act 1

Chapter 1
Lost Without Hope 3
    The Call 6
    The Emergency Room 10
    I See Marcos 14

Chapter 2
The Intensive-Care Unit 19
    Surgery 21
    Luna Arrived 25
    The Military 31

Chapter 3
No Brain Activity 35
    Katelyn Arrived 41
    Unplugged 43

Chapter 4
Back Home 53
    Powerless 55

Chapter 5
The First Date 61
    Engaged 69
    The Wedding 72
    The Honeymoon 76
    Felipe Born 79

Chapter 6
The Funeral 91
    The Burial 95
    My Family Arrived 102
    Reception Say No 104

Act 2

Chapter 7
Back in Albuquerque 113
    Paramedics 115
    Marcos Knew 118

Chapter 8
Good Days 125
    Bad Days 127
    Harley Repaired 129
    No Money 133

Chapter 9
The New Apartment 137
   Fight with Luna 140

Act 3

Chapter 10
I'm Pregnant 147

Chapter 11
I Met Peter 151
   Graduated College 152

Chapter 12
Signs 155
   The First Warning 157
   Married Again 162
   Indigo Born 166

Chapter 13
World Trade Center 171
   The Christmas Gifts 175

Chapter 14
Alchemy 179
   Leaving My Body 186
   Awakening 191
   The Day After 193

Act 4

Chapter 15
Bankruptcy 197
    File for Divorce 203

Chapter 16
Response to my Divorce 209
    The Divorce Papers 214
    Moved to Santa Fe 217

Chapter 17
I Met Jack 221
    Indigo Sick 224

Chapter 18
Began Dating 229
    Moved In 233
    Married Third Time 236

Chapter 19
Began Fighting 239
    The Pattern Repeats 243
    Hernia 250

Chapter 20
Pregnant Viktor 257
    Katelyn and Mom 261

Chapter 21
Spiritual Teachers and Gurus 265

Act 5

Chapter 22
Origin of Pattern 273
   Reflections 277

Chapter 23
Root Cause 283
   The Gift 287

Chapter 24
Shattered Into Being 291

Invocation 301

About the Author 303

Book Summary/Target Audience 305

Contact and Engagements 306

Anne Lamott Quote 307

"You had the power all along; you just had to learn it for yourself."

As proclaimed by: Glenda the good witch in *The Wizard of Oz*.

Act 1

Chapter 1

Lost Without Hope

I tried to focus, to remember where I had been, what I had been doing, only a few hours before. The sun was warm on my skin, a beautiful Spring day, when I pulled into the parking lot and parked the car. It was just before lunchtime when I received the call. Now I was lost, slipping out of my body, no longer tethered to this reality. I searched for signs to lead me back out into the light of day, which no longer existed. The day was forever removed from my grasp.

The hallways of the hospital all looked the same; bright fluorescent lights flickering above, white walls broken by open doors, large squares of industrial linoleum pacing before me, red exit signs at the end of each corridor lighting the way. Nurses in scrubs of varying colors focused on the task at hand, oblivious to my struggle. Hospital beds flashed in my awareness as I passed, leading the way. The smell of disinfectant, urine, sickness and death permeated the air, infecting my memory with its presence.

I had to find my way out, back to where I had been, back to the sunlight of the parking lot. I kept turning, descending down the hallways, struggling to find my way. I could see the parking lot outside through a small window in the door. An empty lot, illuminated by small halos of light in the darkness. I pushed out through the exit into the emptiness. I released the hospital behind me, moving forward into the dark night of my soul.

A storm can only rage for so long before it must relent. The greater the force and the more intense the outpouring, the shorter the time required to unleash its fury. The warm spring day was gone; a cold, black, still night had replaced it. My summer skirt and t-shirt were not enough to shield me from the bitterness of the cold desert night coming on. My body began convulsing, shaking violently, as shock began to take hold of me.

I recognized my car in the distance as the silver gray of my Isuzu Rodeo dimly reflected the light of the nearby lamp towering above. I fixed my sight, determined to escape, and drifted towards the car. I could hear the buzzing hum of the lights overhead, as I passed from darkness to light again and again. I reached for the door, opened the car and clicked the car seat that held Felipe in place. I fumbled into the driver's seat, placing my hands upon the wheel, eyes forward. I could hear my sister Katelyn climb into the passenger seat beside me.

Dazed, fighting to remain in control of my body as it continued to convulse in the cold, I turned the key and the engine fired to life. I slowly backed away from the parking space and began creeping forward – my mind empty, without understanding. Detached, disconnected from awareness, I pressed forward. My life had changed forever in a matter of hours; my family was broken; I was shattered, fractured to the core.

I drove aimlessly through the parking lot, hitting a curb hard. The SUV lurched, banging us from side to side in our seats. My sister was silent, Felipe asleep, as I struggled to hold on. I continued as if in a trance until an exit emerged from the darkness. I released the parking lot behind me in silence, moving forward into the unknown.

I was sinking; the storm had calmed to stillness, a whisper. Awareness of the devastation had begun to penetrate my mind. My soul ripped further from my body, a piece of the storm held forever in the stillness of the void created within me. The rhythmic light, the smell, the texture of the atmosphere created by the storm imprinted itself upon my being. The rest of the storm raged forward, leaving me behind.

I left the parking lot, driving over and through whatever was in front of me. The street unfolded in the darkness. I was driving, we were moving, that was all I knew. My mind was empty, void of purpose or direction. I had no idea where I was going, which road I was on or how to find my way back home. I was lost and it didn't matter anymore. I was numb, floating as the wheels rolled on.

My sister was helpless. She had never been to our new apartment. All she could do was sit silently and bear witness. She asked in her deep voice, steady and calm, "Do you know where you are going?" I answered, "I have no idea," and continued driving. I am certain she was beginning to wonder if we would spend the rest of the night aimlessly wandering the streets of Albuquerque.

I had no internal compass; all I could do was feel if I was moving in the direction of home. I would pause, deciding to continue or to turn, without reason. Waiting, the light red, I looked up and saw a sign I recognized, Lomas Blvd. I knew where I was. I could follow Lomas Blvd. toward the mountain; that would take me home. I could find my way home. I had a focus, a purpose once more.

The Call

Hours earlier, I lay hanging over the edge of the satin couch, black with flashes of silver, burgundy and green, in my living room. I studied Felipe, as he slept soundly in the car seat on the floor beside me. He was so little; his hands and fingers were so tiny next to mine, with a mop of matted black hair on his head, a tinge of yellow to his newborn skin. He was held safe as he slept, wrapped tightly in his swaddling blanket.

Marcos had left for work early. I was alone, sitting in the stillness that surrounded Felipe and me. Nursing him to sleep gave me a feeling of peace, as if we were surrounded in a bubble of protection. The curtains were open, letting the warm Spring sun touch our skin as we soaked up the quiet of the early afternoon light.

I loved my time alone with Felipe. I was free, with no demands, no obligations to fulfill. Our days were spent inside the little world we had created. We would go for short walks in the sun around the neighborhood, returning back to the safety of our home, hidden within the walls.

The phone ringing broke the silence, the bubble, that held us. Felipe remained asleep as I picked up the phone. The call was from the University of New Mexico Hospital, and an emergency-room nurse identified herself on the line. An ambulance had brought someone they couldn't identify into the emergency room. My number was the last one listed on the individual's pager. I knew immediately that it was Marcos. I told the woman, "It's my husband. The pager belongs to my husband."

She denied the possibility, not wanting it to be true. I described his long hair, and his head shaved on the top to display his latest tattoo. I described the tattoos blanketing his body, head, arms, and stomach. Crosses, the lion and the lamb, a wolf and an eagle, a skull wearing a fedora, two angels and a child, all inked into his skin. Three gold teeth crowned his smile. Diamond-studded earrings ran the length of each of ear. The symbol of the date he received Christ, with the month on one ear and the day on the other.

    The nurse again denied it could be him, despite my efforts to confirm. I completed his description as he had left for work, riding his motorcycle. She relented, accepting it must be Marcos; there was nothing left to say. I had to come immediately – those were her last words as she hung up the phone. I stood still for one brief moment, letting the realization sink in. I put the phone down on the couch, as panic began to take hold. I had to go, now.

    Awareness hit me as I looked down. I wasn't dressed to step out the door and into the world. Confused, scared, lost, I had to change my clothes. I was fat, overweight, was all I could think. I had given birth two months before, so nothing fit. I was numb, hurrying to face the lack of self-esteem raging within me. My confidence shrinking, I searched within my closet for something that would fit, something that would make me feel safe.

    I grabbed a summer skirt, loose and non-restricting, to fit the warm spring day, the second of April. I pulled an oversized t-shirt over my head. I grasped for a pair of shoes, my hiking boots. That's what I needed. They were safe. I flung open the dresser drawer searching for wool socks. I pulled the socks on, shoved my feet into the boots and laced them up. I was ready. I raced as fast as I could. I pulled the buckle over Felipe's head and clicked it shut. He was already in his car seat, his favorite napping spot.

I stepped out of the door. The roses were in bloom on the porch; their scent touched me, unconscious in the moment. It was a beautiful day. I clicked the car seat into place and climbed into the car. I was uncertain, as the direction to the University of New Mexico Hospital was unclear in my mind. Felipe was born at Lovelace Hospital, close to our house. The University of New Mexico Hospital was the only Level One Trauma Center in the state of New Mexico, and it was close to downtown.

I knew it was near the university, so I headed in that direction. I moved forward without knowing, hoping for signs to show me the way to the Emergency Room. As I got closer, I followed the small hospital signs along the road, with the big H, to the entrance. I told the parking attendant that my husband had been brought in by ambulance a few minutes earlier. He handed me a pass, placing it on the dashboard of my car, and told me to park near the booth in the first row of cars.

The Emergency Room doors loomed ahead of me. I knew someone would help me once I got inside. I just had to get through the doors, and everything would be okay. I lifted the car seat onto my forearm with Felipe snuggled inside. As I entered through the automatic doors, I announced to the receptionist, "I'm here to see my husband. The ambulance just brought him in. I received a call from a nurse telling me to come immediately." My voice was weak, beginning to break – my chest exploding – as I tried to hold back the tears raging within. Terrified, I reached out for help, my voice giving way, the emotion flooding outward, revealing my fear. The kindness in her voice, the compassion in her eyes made me feel safe, causing all of my emotions concealed within to rush to the surface.

The Emergency Room

An attendant appeared at my side and whisked me back to a room by myself. I took a moment, allowing the situation to form around me. The stroller was in the room with me. I didn't remember getting it out, putting Felipe in or pushing it through the emergency-room doors. The room was small, cramped, with the oversized stroller. The walls were painted white. There was a brown laminate-topped table with black metal legs in the center of the room. A gray metal folding chair was pushed beneath the table and an old rotary telephone sat waiting for me.

I was supposed to call friends and family; someone would be back soon to tell me more. I was alone again, with Felipe sound asleep. I had no phone numbers, no address book on hand – I couldn't call Marcos' family. Then I remembered that I had memorized Marcos' mom's number. I called; the phone rang and his brother Val answered. I asked him to call the family, "Let everyone know that Marcos has been in a motorcycle accident, and it's bad. I don't know anything – you'd better come now." He hung up. I called my mom, telling her where I was and what I knew. "I don't have any answers. I don't know what's happening; no one here is talking to me." I hung up the phone. I'd been forgotten in this room without windows, cut off, separated from the outside.

I waited, sitting quietly and holding my breath, as the door opened. I was handed a bag of Marcos' belongings. A clear plastic bag. No explanation, just the bag and a promise that someone would be in soon to talk with me. The nurse was gone as quickly as he'd arrived, the door banging shut behind him. I sat for a moment, looking at the contents of the bag through the clear plastic. I could see the clothes that Marcos was wearing when he left the house. I hesitated, staring at the bag, and not wanting to know what it held – not wanting this journey to begin. I was not ready to sort through my husband's belongings.

I slowly unwound the plastic, untwisting the seal that held this moment inside. As the bag opened, it released the trauma. The smell of my husband's accident seeped into the room, mixed with the scent of his cologne. I recognized the distinctive scent of his presence, as the pure Aveda fragrance vainly attempted to cover the horror beneath.

The room filled with the scent of the street, covered in oil and gas. The smell of fresh blood filled my nostrils, along with that of clean clothes turned to rags covered in grease. My hands felt the damp, sticky, residue that remained. I studied the jagged edge that the shears had made as they cut quickly through his black jeans and t-shirt. I felt and smelled the mixture of blood and oil that the clothes held in the fiber of their being; the black fabric hiding the truth just beyond my vision. The rags felt heavy, hanging limply in my hand, filled with the blood they had absorbed, giving texture to once-smooth cotton.

Trauma was with me now, present within the room. Fear enveloped me, marking me with its scent. I could feel it sinking deep into the pit of my stomach. I felt my throat tightening, choking back what was to come. I placed the clothes back in the bag, gently folding the pieces as best I could. I pressed them down, pushing the emotions rising within me down with them.

I saw Marcos' black address book nestled with his belongings, tucked to the side of the bag. I pulled it out. It was clean and untouched by the accident. I opened it, searching for more numbers to call. I dialed his uncle who lived close by in Albuquerque. He answered, saying, "We already know. There's no need to call anyone else." I was told, "Val's called everyone. We're on our way."

I was alone, isolated without connection, no voice to express what I was experiencing, no one to reach out to. I was lost; I couldn't find myself in the midst of this storm raining down on me. It came out of nowhere. I was unprepared, resting with Felipe, hidden within the safety of our walls. Now I sat without sound, in the void of this small space, lost in nothingness.

All I was told was that they were coming. Someone would be with me soon. The family was coming from Taos, Santa Fe and Albuquerque. It would take time. I had to be calm, hold it all in, wait and trust. My eyes fell on Felipe, as he continued to sleep soundly. He was sheltered from it all, unconscious, separated from this world I was experiencing. My eyes found peace studying him, slowing down my mind, washing away my fears.

I couldn't cry. I had to believe. I had to have faith, hold on to hope. I didn't know what was happening. All I knew was that Marcos was safe here. He was in the hospital; the nurses and doctors were doing everything they could to help him. I had to trust, to hold onto Marcos in my mind. I couldn't surrender hope or give in to tears of desperation. I had to hold on. I had to wait for someone to rescue me from this room, from this moment.

I See Marcos

A nurse came, gently opening the door, and asked, "Would you like to see Marcos?" I said, "Yes, of course." I lifted Felipe from the car seat, picking him up as carefully as I could, so as not to wake him. As I carried him, holding him tightly in my arms, he roused only slightly. We walked down a white hall, through swinging double doors and into a long room filled with activity. It was a hub for the doctors and nurses in the emergency wing, as they rushed from curtain to curtain.

I followed the nurse, staying close on her heels, when a doctor stopped me. He turned to the nurse and asked her to take the baby, telling her I couldn't carry him in with me. He didn't address me. He didn't ask me if this was all right. I didn't want to let Felipe go. He was all I had, my safety. I didn't know this nurse or this doctor. The hospital was filled with people. I didn't trust for my newborn son to be taken from me here. I didn't know if he would be returned to me safely. I was supposed to be his protector. The nurse gently pulled him from my arms, reassuring me it would be all right. I had no choice.

My world was collapsing; all that I loved was being stripped away. They were afraid that the shock would be too great, that when I entered the room to be with Marcos, I would drop my baby. They thought I would drop Felipe on the floor. They were anticipating that I would scream, wail, collapse in agony. I looked into the small, windowless room filled with darkness, outside of the bright lights focused like lasers upon Marcos' body. "The doctors are working on him – there will be a lot of blood, so be prepared," were the last words I heard as I entered the space, meeting this moment head on.

Marcos lay unconscious on a slab, naked with sheets draped across his privates. Bloody pieces of cloth were strewn like rags where he lay, and on the floor beneath him, in this makeshift surgical room. I could see a vain attempt to clean up, wipe away the evidence, the pools of blood that foreshadowed what was to come, before I entered. Doctors and nurses crowded around him in a ring, opening only narrowly for me to see as I approached.

I stepped directly to Marcos' side, through the small opening, reaching into the trauma with my hand, grasping for my husband's shoulder, and gently resting my hand upon his clammy skin. My voice calm, comforting, as I steadied myself with a smile, I said, "Don't be afraid, Marcos. Everything will be all right. God rose Lazarus from the dead, he can do the same for you. You are safe, God can raise you up again. Don't be afraid, Marcos, everything will be okay."

The doctors were uncertain, confused by my reaction. The woman I had been earlier had disappeared, and something else had stepped in: a survivor. I was confident, strong, resolute in my conviction that Marcos would be raised up, healed and made whole. I didn't scream, or cry out to God, asking why this was happening. I didn't collapse upon the blood-covered floor, writhing in agony the way they'd anticipated. I spoke in a calm and powerful voice, defying what I was witnessing before me. The doctors didn't understand my response – it was startling for them to hear. Cutting me off, they pushed me out of the room, fearing the words coming from my mouth.

"They are taking him to the intensive-care unit upstairs," I was told as they moved on, leaving me behind. I became aware, standing in the hub of the emergency room, that my bowels had released. I had soiled my pants without being aware of it. The trauma had been so extreme that my mind could not hold it; my body could not contain it. I had severed the part of my soul that could not be present in that moment. My root, my connection with the Earth, the foundation of my being had been shaken to the core. That which could not hold, could not withstand the intensity of this experience, was broken and released.

A new strength took root deep within me. The cord buried within my heart, connecting me to the Source of all life, twanged with the tension of my focus. The part of me that was weak, that grasped in fear, was gone – disconnecting me from who I had been only moments before in the waiting room. I had been pushed beyond my limits into the unlimited potential of who I am meant to be. The energy of life, the power of love, flowed into me, allowing me to move forward into the hall and to continue moving into this experience.

I stood, holding my newborn son again in my arms. No one noticed, only I knew that everything had shifted. I had stepped into that room, laid my hand upon Marcos, with the strength of God within me. No doubt, no hesitation, only strength and declaration of the unlimited power and potential that is God, the Source of all life within me.

I became the calm in the eye of the storm, the stillness in chaos. In that moment I owned my power, and I felt it flow through me into Marcos. The storm was taking form. It had come from nowhere, and it wasn't done with me yet. The sky had been blue, filled with soft, floating clouds of pure white, laced with the scent of roses. In an instant there was blackness enveloping the light, the scent of blood overwhelming my being. The storm raged in full force, pelting my tender skin, hurling blows from the heavens.

I walked, holding Felipe close to me, following the nurse back out through the swinging double doors, back to the small room, back to my past without life, without hope, filled with fear. I asked no questions, my voice silent. I had released that part of me that couldn't be present. It had escaped out through the root of my being, my connection to this world. I struggled now to maintain my new strength with the scent of trauma still lingering in this space. Shut off, isolated again, I squeezed Felipe close to my chest, fighting to hold the energy of love within me. I held my sanctuary in my arms, my refuge in the storm, with all my might.

Marcos' family arrived. I was numb. I can't remember who pulled me from my small cell, maybe Larry, Marcos' favorite uncle, who was more like a brother to him. I have no memory of that time, no awareness to pull from. I was vacillating between who I had been moments before and who I was becoming. A void had been created within me as my identity was stripped away. I was left untethered, my wounds raw. I was drifting, floating through time and space, without limit to the suffering that could be unleashed, without limit to the love that could unfold through me.

Chapter 2

The Intensive-Care Unit

People began arriving one after the other. Somehow they all seemed to know more of what was happening than I did. They had information. They had answers and explanations. I had seen Marcos, but I had no words to connect what I had seen with any understanding. I was guided to the waiting room upstairs, designated for the families of those in the ICU. We all gathered there – with me in my skirt, hiking boots, wool socks and poop in my pants, holding Felipe in my arms.

I took a moment to collect myself, pull myself together, check in and see if I was still in this body, still willing to move forward, to experience what was happening around me. I went to the bathroom and cleaned up as best I could. I removed my soiled underwear, my symbol of releasing who I had been. I paused, grasping to catch up to what was happening now within me.

I looked myself square in the eyes, in the small, single bathroom mirror, and spoke to God. I prayed that everything would be all right. I confessed my fear, my desperation, my resolute belief in the power of the Almighty, the infinite resources of All that is. I cried out, releasing it all, asking Marcos to be healed, returned home once more. I was scared, alone, in the midst of Marcos' family and friends. I confessed my true feelings to God only, looking into my own eyes. I placed faith in the hands of hope, assuming the outcome to be what I believed it must be.

I said not a word of my fears, of the soiled underpants, that I'd left behind. Not a word of my trauma, my weakness, my crying out. I stepped into my new strength and allowed the energy of life and of love to flow through me once more. I smiled and comforted those who were present in the waiting room – those waiting for word about Marcos, and also those who had their own loved ones in the ICU waiting for words of hope and encouragement.

This was not my experience, not my drama and heartache. I had shattered, and only the light within me remained in this moment. I was a witness to the suffering around me. I was no longer tied to the experience of suffering. My heart was filled with love, a deep compassion and appreciation for those present. I was the support, the comforter of those who were broken.

I rose above, escaped my own experience. I left my own thoughts, fears and doubts far below my awareness. I looked outward, beyond myself. I saw others breaking beside me, and reached out to help and to serve. In the process I was made stronger, more at peace within my own heart. Their need outweighed my own. Their pain and sorrow was real at this time; mine had been removed from my being, from my awareness, as I began the process of transformation deep within.

My mom and grandpa called me on my cell phone to tell me that everyone back home, in upstate New York, was praying for Marcos, and for the doctors' hands to be guided. My mom told me of people from long ago, from my childhood, who were praying for us, praying for Marcos to be well. I was comforted by this outpouring of love.

My heart broke open with the love I was receiving, that was flowing through me, a love far greater than I could ever grasp. I was grateful for the loving kindness of those who cried out to help, to heal the suffering of those they had never met. I was touched by those whose hearts were broken in the hour of need. They reached out in prayer, sending waves of love without limit in my direction.

Surgery

A young doctor motioned for me to step out into the hall, separate from everyone else. He explained that they needed to perform an experimental surgery to help Marcos. It was risky, so they needed my signed consent, giving permission to perform the surgery. I wasn't sure what the risks were; I can't remember if they ever even covered the risks. I knew I needed to sign for the doctors to move forward, for Marcos to receive their help. I was focused on Marcos, and the fact that he needed surgery – and that I was required to sign a release for him to receive it. I would do anything the doctors requested, if it would bring Marcos back to me.

The only news I received when they asked me to sign the release form was that the pressure was building in Marcos' head, and it had to be relieved. I asked no questions, only listened. The blood was pooling, crushing the brain beneath the force of the swelling. I said yes to the surgery. I signed the papers without hesitation. The doctor raced back to Marcos, leaving me behind.

A hole was drilled in the back of Marcos' head to relieve the pressure, to save his brain. I had no concept of time, no awareness of the shift that was occurring, forever changing who I am. I didn't understand what anyone was telling me. I had been swept up by the storm. I trusted that they were doing all they could to save Marcos. I sat empty, spinning, whirling, coming in and out of reality, as I waited.

I felt confident that everything would be all right. We had prayed, cried out to God for his help and healing. I had no reason to believe that anything other than a miracle would take place. Everything always worked out for the best. My hope remained undiminished by thoughts of doubt. My belief and expectation of what a miracle looked like was fixed within my heart. I placed all power, all responsibility outside of my own hands and into the hands of God.

I sat holding Felipe, silently waiting, as I briefly became aware of the clothing I thought was appropriate to wear to shield me as I stepped outside the door. I looked down at the combination of items I had selected to give me security and confidence. I became self-conscious, embarrassed, for one brief moment. I was ashamed of what I looked like, compared to those around me. I had no identity. I was a mismatched mess of flowery innocence and hiking readiness. I had protected myself as the good girl, while simultaneously being ready to run to the safety of the mountain at any moment.

More people continued to arrive, offering support and prayers. I was conscious of how I must have appeared in their eyes – a twenty-two-year-old, stay-at-home mom struggling to finish the last classes of my degree with a two-month-old son asleep in my arms. I had come to New Mexico to complete my Bachelor of Fine Arts, in Studio Arts, at the University of New Mexico. I had transferred from SUNY Purchase, a New York State college, at the age of twenty. I was young, a newly married mom, new to New Mexico, new to this family and these friends.

I was told I could go see Marcos, now that the surgery was over. I asked again, "Can Felipe come with me? Marcos is his father. Please let me bring him with me. Marcos will want to see him." The answer was the same – "No." Knowing I must go alone, I followed the nurse down the long corridor of the intensive-care unit, to Marcos' room.

I told myself that everything would be all right. I knew it would be now. And when I saw that Marcos was in room seventeen, my hope was confirmed. He would be fine. This was my lucky number. I was born on September 17th. This was my sign that everything would be okay.

I stepped into the room. Marcos was wrapped in a white cotton sheet, with a warm white blanket on top. Everything was clean, calm and quiet. No blood was visible. The nurses had created a beautiful space for healing. I was grateful. I placed my hands on Marcos, and began speaking to him from my heart. I told him, "Marcos, I'm here. I love you. Everything will be all right. All your family is here. They came right away. They all love you so much." I talked with him as though nothing was different, as if he was awake and listening to every word I spoke. Nothing had happened, nothing had changed. My mind could only accept that everything would be fine, that Marcos would wake up and come home.

Luna Arrived

I became aware that someone else was coming. I could hear Luna, Marcos' mom, coming down the hall, her steps slapping the floor beneath her feet. I could hear the fierceness in her voice as she warned those standing close to her to let her pass. They gave way, as everyone always did who stood in her path. She was small, not even five feet tall, with piercing green eyes, made so by colored contacts. Her hair was dyed a fiery purplish red, extending outward from her head in small spikes. I could see she was exploding within; fighting to hold the emotion, the rage, boiling within her.

I couldn't relate to her demeanor. Marcos was going to be fine; there was nothing to be upset about. We were with him – he was not alone. We would help him to recover, to rehabilitate. I was filled with the certainty of my hope, as I spoke to Marcos, smiling, "Your mom is here, isn't that great? She made it. She is beside you now." Luna's eyes tore at my skin.

She couldn't understand. She couldn't relate or connect to me. In her eyes, my behavior seemed bizarre. I didn't make any sense to her. I appeared callous, uncaring, indifferent to the fate of her son. She saw me as incapable of being present – unable to witness what was happening – to see it for what it was and accept it.

What she didn't realize was that the part of me that couldn't accept this experience, this trauma, had slipped away – and the survivor had stepped in. In that moment in the emergency room, when I first laid eyes on Marcos, I stepped forward in power. I became grounded, moving from my connection to Source, acting in the moment. I had soiled my underpants in the process of releasing all that was too weak to stand in the light of this truth.

The breaking of my being, of my soul, left me feeling etheric, untethered, floating through space. I had become an open channel for the energy and power of love to flow through me. A void had been created within me, and all that remained to fill it was light. All I could see – all I could allow to flow through me – was light. It was the only way I could survive being in this body through this experience. I had disconnected from the harshness of suffering and had stepped into the power and the safety of the Divine. This allowed me to float in a place of faith, of hope – a place of joyous expectation and belief in the miracle that I believed was to come. I surrendered, and I handed over my trust, believing in the perfection of All that is.

I was certain of the outcome I expected. I was not afraid. I pulled away from Luna's intensity. She was deep in the heart of suffering, with a great darkness enveloping her. She had accepted a reality that was harsh – without hope – and a great loss permeated her entire being. It was too great for me to bear. I returned to the safety of Felipe in my arms in the waiting area. I escaped the darkness of the trauma surrounding Luna.

I was only able to visit Marcos for brief moments. I was torn between holding my newborn son enveloped in love, keeping him safe, or staying at my husband's bedside as he lay unconscious. Luna never left him, except for brief moments as I entered the room. As I left she returned, or I left as she returned. We did not occupy the same space for very long. We were not unkind to one another; it was a polarity, an opposing magnetism that separated us beyond consciousness.

We were the extreme opposite expressions of being in this moment – the divergence of light and darkness. Both expressions were equally valid; we survived the experience differently, that's all. The nurses and staff of the ICU would not allow me to bring Felipe into the ICU. They had a policy that would not allow infants or young children to enter. I survived by creating a space of love and peace for my son. Luna survived by holding all of her suffering within for her son. We each had a purpose we were fulfilling, a purpose we believed in with our entire being.

I sat in the waiting room in the midst of Marcos' friends and family and reflected upon my arrival at this moment. I sank into the isolation of protection and let my thoughts drift to how different I was from those around me, sitting in this space. I looked at myself in contrast to those in the waiting room. I was a young, white – not Hispanic – girl from back East in upstate New York. I had no familiarity with their culture, customs or traditions. I came from a small family with a Baptist upbringing, raised near a traditional Amish community.

My upbringing always made Marcos laugh. I grew up making my own butter, drinking raw milk and eating fresh-made cheese. We butchered our own chickens, provided by our Amish neighbors. We got our eggs from my best friend, who lived next door. We grew our own vegetables in a one-acre garden at my grandparents' house down the street. All our food was homemade; there were no coffee shops or restaurants. The grocery store was more of a gas station/convenience store than a full-service grocery store. Next door to the grocery store were the fire department and a small local museum in an old house. Across the street was the feed store for the animals.

The thoughts streaming into my mind allowed me to justify my belief that I was different, separate and alone. I was foreign to them in every way – their way of speaking, the foods they ate, how they communicated with each other. They ate red chile on their mashed potatoes, not gravy. They offered twice-cooked, or burnt, oatmeal for breakfast. They made tamales by hand in batches of one hundred or more. They ate meat pastries or prune pies for dessert.

Shattered Into Being

Nearly all their foods were identified by Spanish names. It was as if I was an exchange student, studying abroad.

When they spoke they used their lips, pursing them together, jutting their chin out to point. They would add elongated vowels to the end of words and make sing song sounds, unique to Northern New Mexico, in conversation. The sounds would rise in pitch and resonate from the nasal cavity. Sometimes an entire conversation would unfold from just these sounds and facial gestures. At points they would mix Spanish and English together – for example, "Bueno Bye." I was constantly double-checking what was going on, never quite certain of what was being communicated.

Marcos loved to hear stories of my family, and he adored my Grandpa Henry – though he would routinely hang up on my grandpa because he spoke so slowly. The phone would ring, and Marcos would say, "Hello, Hello?" then hang up. When the phone would ring a second time, immediately after, he would answer the phone laughing and say, "I'm sorry, Grandpa Henry, I didn't realize you were on the line."

Marcos and I had been married for less than a year. Now, as his wife, I was responsible for the decisions regarding his life and well-being. The doctors spoke with me and sought direction. I was the responsible party at twenty-two years old. I couldn't even find my way across town. Now I was signing papers for surgeries – and I couldn't possibly comprehend the dangers of performing them.

My thoughts brought me back to the moment, with feelings of separation lingering within me. My mind now infected, I found solace as the victim. I made myself believe there was no one to support me. They were all supporting Luna. She was a part of their family, and to them, her behavior was understandable. I was smiling and saying how great it was that the family was all here, as if we were having a party and I was glad to see that everyone could make it. Luna was visibly angry, in the throes of grief and turmoil. She showed the outward signs of confusion, desperation and frustration. I was seen as a child playing make-believe. This was not how people behaved in these circumstances. I couldn't help it. I had shifted. I wasn't the same anymore. A transformation was in progress, whether I understood it or not.

To protect myself, I pushed everyone outside my walls, the barriers I had created. I made myself an outsider as I drifted away in thought, Felipe asleep in my arms. I kept the narrative running in my mind, reflecting back, as I surrendered to Marcos' belief in the power of God. He had seen and experienced miracles of God's love many times. He had been a rebellious youth, having joined the army at seventeen. Going AWOL multiple times, he dealt in arms trading, and he both used and sold illicit drugs. Though he was captured on several occasions, he managed to escape discipline. And somehow, he would run off to various parts of Europe – only to return to the military – and then disappear again.

The Military

Marcos was always lucky, escaping drug raids in Germany, and jumping out of a second-story window to escape being court-martialed. He even flew back to the US on a military aircraft, avoiding detection, until it was too late. He escaped back to his home in Taos, New Mexico, to lose himself in the far reaches of the mountains of the southwest.

Addicted, broken, suffering from hepatitis B with his liver shutting down, Marcos returned home. The local doctor wrote him off for dead, without hope. His skin was yellowed beyond repair. He walled himself off in a little room in his grandma's house. Mama Mercy, as he called her. He grew up under her care, so Grandma Mercy became Mama Mercy.

Marcos hung black blankets over the windows to block out the blinding light, resigning himself to the withdrawals of addiction. His body shaking and convulsing, at the edge of death for over a week, Marcos experienced a miracle. He heard a voice, an angel's voice as he told it, telling him, "Do not be afraid. You are not alone. You will be healed. You will live." He saw a presence of light in the small, blackened room, and knew the words were not coming from within his head, or from the hallucinations of withdrawal. In that moment, faith was born – awakened – within his heart. He awoke the next morning and removed the blankets from the windows. The crisis had passed, and his body was renewing once again. He would not die, just as the angel had predicted. He would heal and live a new life dedicated to God.

Once strong, he turned himself in to military authorities to face his sentence. Relieved he would not be held at Leavenworth Penitentiary, but at one of the nearby forts instead, Marcos served his time, missing Thanksgiving and Christmas with his family. He was never caught or charged with gun or drug running. He served time only for going AWOL. He was not even twenty at the time, as he had entered the military before his eighteenth birthday.

Remembering Marcos' past, I was unfazed by what was happening in the ICU at this moment. Marcos had survived many times, experienced many miracles. This would be yet another story of the power of God's grace. I remained with Felipe, waiting in the lounge. I was confident Marcos would be fine, and I knew Felipe needed me.

I continued to speak words of faith, encouragement and support to those who had loved ones in the ICU. My heart went out to them and their tragedies. I smiled, and I expressed kindness and support to those who shared this space. I believed my situation was different; we were going to be spared the fate that they feared. I felt alive – empowered by faith – focused on hope and the outcome I anticipated.

I was calm, centered, at peace. I had seen Marcos resting peacefully in his room. There were no visible signs of trauma; no scarring, bruising or blood. I was surrounded by the power of prayer, and I felt love coursing through my veins. I knew Marcos would be fine, that everything would be perfect. It always had been. I was Pollyanna to a T, and no doubt could touch my faith.

I expressed my gratitude for the paramedics, that Marcos was going to be all right because they had responded so quickly. He had the best doctors and was in the best medical facility in the state. Everyone was praying for a miracle. The doctors would take care of Marcos. I felt surrounded by a bubble of light. I was happy; my heart was at peace. I wouldn't feel this way if he wasn't going to be okay.

I accepted my beliefs and feelings as truth. They had to be true. I was at peace, surrounded by the presence of God. I was feeling a miracle in the making. At times I was almost giddy with excitement, secretly anticipating the news I expected to hear: "Marcos has overcome all odds. He has made a miraculous recovery, and he'll be going home soon." He was in room seventeen – that was my sign, my validation. All I needed to do was wait.

Chapter 3

No Brain Activity

My thoughts shifted. I was sitting alone, in a room filled with people, as Felipe rested quietly in my arms. It was as if he was aware of the suffering unfolding around him, filling the halls of the hospital with hopelessness. He chose to escape into sleep instead of being present. He barely moved, and he hadn't cried once since we entered the hospital. As I looked around the waiting room, I realized how lost I had gotten, how disconnected from myself I had become before this moment.

I was jolted back to the moment at hand, as another doctor I had not yet met requested that I step out into the hall, separate from everyone else. He was courteous and professional, businesslike and to the point. He told me his title and what tests he had run. He stated, in a matter-of-fact tone, that he did not see any activity on Marcos' CAT scans – no brain activity at all.

I looked at him and acknowledged what he was saying. I had no idea what it meant, what he was trying to communicate to me. He waited for a reaction – some response – an acknowledgment of comprehension to sweep across my face. There was none. His words had no value; I received no information from what he was telling me.

I was in a place of hope and optimism. His words fell on deaf ears. His warnings went unheeded. I didn't understand the ramifications of what he was saying. "There's no activity" was all I heard, as if he were saying "We are standing in the hallway right now." A statement of fact, without the emotion necessary to relay the outcome. He was kind and did not push. He delivered the news, waited and moved on.

He didn't tell me what it meant to have no more brain activity. For all I knew, it was confirmation that Marcos was not conscious. To him it was evident; to me, it made no sense. It had no impact. I needed it spelled out; an analogy or story for comprehension, which never came. I didn't understand, and I didn't ask for understanding. I said thank you and returned to my seat on the couch – waiting again for the healing I was anticipating.

The forecast had been delivered. A life-threatening storm was on the horizon. Preparations were to be made, life put in order. I went along my way, as if going on a picnic. No wonder they stared at me in confusion – waiting for the shock, horror and fear that never came. All the normal responses to what was happening had been stripped from me, and I was the person responsible for making the life-altering decisions.

A third doctor entered the waiting room, requesting that I step out into the hall once again. He was curt and brisk as he led the way to the spot in the hallway where he felt we could talk. I believe he was the lead doctor for the intensive-care unit. He wanted to speak with me privately. I stood, looking into his face. I could see that he was angry with me; frustrated, upset. I could see it in his face and hear it in his words as they tumbled out abruptly and without warmth.

I didn't understand why he was mad at me. I had never met him, never laid eyes on him before this moment. I listened to the judgment in his voice, as he declared in a statement of fact, "You are cruel, insensitive and uncaring. It is heartless to leave your husband on life support. He has no brain activity. This is wrong. You need to let him go." I was confused, shocked by his words that were slapping me in the face. By the self-righteous condemnation pouring out of him, validating the superiority of his verdict.

I had made no decisions, told the doctors nothing. All I had done was listen when they pulled me aside. Nothing had been requested of me, no action, no decision. The last doctor told me the news and left. He didn't ask for any decision to be made. I never told him that Marcos must remain on life support, with no hope of recovery. This was how the news was delivered to me. This was how I came to understand that my husband would not be returning home.

I was young; my self-esteem and confidence were lacking from years of neglect. I couldn't advocate for myself or Marcos. The doctor's words sprayed over me, crushing me. I was silent. I said nothing. I didn't defend myself from the venom biting into my flesh through his words. I didn't cry out and reprimand him for his insensitivity and cruelty. I stood silent, looking into his eyes. Numb, I turned and walked back to the waiting room.

I became the gap between moments. The silence after the thunder. No flash of lightning to declare and make evident the injustice rendered unto me. The storm raged within unseen, unheard, even by me. It hid behind the awareness of my mind, in the deep recesses of my being, to remain hidden for years to come.

My spirit momentarily removed from my physical form, I reached out for Felipe and held him close to me. He was life, hope, love. I looked at him and escaped. I was transformed back into a nurturing mother, separate from all that surrounded me. No one said a word. No one asked me what the doctor had said. No one sought to comfort me, to reach me deep behind the veil.

I waited for news that Marcos would be fine, with rehabilitation, that we could return home as a family. Denial took hold of me. I didn't seek out further information. I couldn't accept or integrate into my psyche any of what I was hearing. I remained steadfast, reinforced by the signs and faith that I had placed outside of myself. Removing my experience with the last doctor from my memory, I continued moving into this moment.

In retrospect, I believe that the last doctor had been communicating with Marcos' family. Luna would never give up, or allow Marcos to be taken off life support. She would have him on life support for the rest of his life, believing he would wake up one day. Her love was powerful, deep and intense. She could not imagine a world without her eldest son. He was her best friend. The doctor was reacting to her defiance, her desire to hold on without acknowledgment of his counsel, when he attacked me. I was annihilated for *her* fight, for *her* daring to defy him.

I wasn't even in the same room. It didn't matter whether the cross was mine to bear; it was my decision to make. The doctor believed I was the one. He attacked me as the source. I was ignorant of the family conversations, isolated from them. They were gathering information, speaking to the doctors and nurses, advocating for Marcos. I was sitting quietly, holding Felipe close to me, as a life preserver in the waiting room. I was disconnected by my own choice – torn between being at my husband's side and protecting my son. I chose to be with my son; it was safe and peaceful with him. Marcos was surrounded by suffering, drama and conflict.

I left Felipe and walked down the corridor to see Marcos again. I paused and looked closely as I entered his room. I could see under the blankets that something was not right with his hips. One leg was longer than the other, and the angle was off; his head was swollen and puffy. Otherwise, he looked as though he was sleeping. His injuries on the surface appeared minor. There were no cuts, abrasions or broken bones. There was no horror to look upon, as I had seen in the emergency room. The nurses had created the illusion of serenity and peace in the midst of chaos. I wanted desperately to believe in the illusion, to throw aside the doctors' words. Reality no longer matched what I was witnessing, or wanted to believe.

I talked with Marcos then, as if he were awake and present in conversation with me. This was easy for me. I had spent my life alone in the woods, talking to plants, trees and animals. I was at ease speaking with those who could not answer me in words to be heard with my ears. I communicated from my heart, and I heard with my heart all that needed to be said. I reassured Marcos that he was safe, and that the doctors were doing everything they could to help him. I told him that I would stand beside him and help him walk again. We would make it through this. It would be all right. This was the only outcome I could accept – all that I could embrace – my only focus.

A nurse pulled me aside, out into the hallway of his room. She assured me that they could pump Marcos up with morphine before they would take him off the machines. He would be free, and there would be no pain. The decision had been made. I accepted by not resisting, not speaking up, not questioning by whose authority the decision had been declared. I was defeated. Hope no longer sustained me; my certainty was removed. Marcos' fate was now beyond my control.

Katelyn Arrived

I looked down the hall, past the nurse, to see my sister Katelyn walking confidently towards me, dressed as usual all in black. I felt a sense of relief wash over me, as my knees nearly buckled at the sight of her. Katelyn was strong, decisive and powerful. She was a force to be reckoned with in words, physical strength and stature. Her presence was palpable; without saying a word, she communicated a position of authority. She let no one take her voice, disregard her or walk over her. She was a grounding force, bringing solidity to the moment. I knew I could assume that her strength would help magnify the strength within me. I could survive this moment, through her power, hiding in her certainty. I had done it all my life.

Katelyn had been at work when she heard the news about the accident from my mom. She was living in New York City at the time, working in high-end retail. She told her boss what had happened after she received the call. She was well respected at work, and she never took vacations or left early unless it was absolutely necessary. Upon hearing the news, her boss told her to take cash from the register and go straight to the airport, immediately. She could take any clothes from the store she needed, but she had to go now. He told her to get in the car and go – and that's exactly what she did.

She went straight to the airport and told the airlines that there had been an accident; she had to get to Albuquerque International Airport *right now;* and she needed a seat on the next flight out. They got her a seat, and she was on her way. Katelyn had always been self-reliant, with a commanding presence, since childhood. She was more of a parent to me than a sister only two years older. It was nothing for her to declare what she needed, and expect it to be so. A seat on the next flight out, if she needed it, was simply a matter of fact.

Katelyn landed, hailed a taxi and told the driver, "Take me to the University of New Mexico Hospital; my brother-in-law has been in an accident." She made it from New York City to Albuquerque, New Mexico in record time. My sister was by my side, standing with me, when I needed her most. I knew I would be safe with her beside me. I could accept what was happening with Katelyn present. She faced reality and dealt with it, in all situations, with little to no emotion revealed on her exterior.

She stood next to me, by Marcos' bed, and held my hand. The room was calm. The rhythmic pulsing of the machines was comforting to me. The machine that pumped life into Marcos' body was steady, constant and reassuring. There was no rush. No reason for anything to change. No need to alter what was working. I couldn't understand the importance, the urgency, of shutting off the machines right now. What would it hurt to continue pumping life into Marcos' body?

We stood silently watching. Katelyn asked me no questions. She had heard what the nurse shared with me and knew that it was the end. We watched as Marcos' chest artificially inflated, the air forced into his lungs. We waited as others began to enter the room and stand around Marcos' body in a circle, as the nurse in the corner stayed by the machine.

Unplugged

Another nurse came in and placed needles into the IV bag, pumping an extra dose of morphine into Marcos' body. The nurse waited for the drugs to enter

Marcos' bloodstream, as the clock ticked away the minutes. The machines rhythmically pumped the beat of his heart out loud. The lead nurse continued to stand by in the corner, ready to release the machines. He waited a moment longer before notifying us that the machines would stop, and Marcos would be forced to breathe on his own. He said, "Marcos' life will be in his own hands once the machines stop." That was it – the two-minute warning – called out loud.

The machines stopped. We all watched. It was as if time moved in slow motion, and simultaneously speeded up, with the focus of our intent for Marcos' breath to continue. Marcos' chest slowly rose half way, and sank. The last partial breath was given to him by the machine. It pumped through his lungs with half the force, and slipped away. It was done. It was that fast, and that slow – and it was over. No struggle, no fight. No breath, no movement. His body was still. Marcos had been gone long before the machines began to falsify his life.

Marcos was gone, never once having opened his eyes to the awareness of this experience. Never once having witnessed what was surrounding him, who was present, who was broken by his loss. The monitors lost the rhythmic beat, the pulse of his life. This was replaced by a flatline, and a high-pitched buzzing – the shrill sound of death interrupting. The black of the darkened window, stark against the white of the hospital wall, was burned into my memory. That was the record that my mind would keep of the end – Marcos' final moments – a black, shiny void on the wall, breaking the white surrounding it.

There was no presence lingering in the room. He was gone. The room was still, silent, empty. The reassuring, rhythmic sound was gone. The shrill buzzing sound of warning had quieted. All that remained was the ticking of the clock above his bed, recording the end, documenting the facts at hand. The nurse had pulled the plug and it was recorded. The room was to be made ready for the next story of tragedy or triumph. Marcos' soul had left with ease, as if it had been waiting for the machines to quiet and release us all from this moment in which we, too, had become trapped.

Marcos was peaceful, as he rested in the warm bed, covered in clean, fresh blankets. I was blinded to everything else. Only pieces remain in my memory, revealed to me in glimpses through time and space. It all happened so quickly. The nurses knew that Marcos had no ability to breathe on his own; no chance to sustain his life without the help of the machines. He had no life in him, no breath, no heartbeat remaining. It was the machines all along. The rush, the urgency had been to enable the rest of us to accept this fact. It was an impatience for us to move on, to make the room available and bring it all to an end.

I was never allowed to have Felipe with me, even at the end, as his father passed away. Policy prohibited it, not even to say goodbye. Felipe never made a sound. He never cried or fussed once through this whole experience. Felipe remained silent despite it all, as if comforted by an unseen hand.

All I knew was that Katelyn was beside me. She had made it just in time. I wasn't alone. I watched as Marcos slipped away, and I wasn't alone. I was adrift, the winds of change moving me, altering my course without my knowing or understanding. Marcos had stopped where he lay. I didn't understand what had happened. I had prayed, the signs had been given – and this was the outcome?

We continued to stand in a circle around Marcos. There were no words said, no ceremony of any kind. No acknowledgment of his passing spoken out loud. Silently, one by one, we stepped out of the room. I stepped into the hallway with Katelyn at my side. She asked if I was all right, and I nodded yes. The nurses came up and hugged me, saying how sorry they were that they couldn't save him. They held me close, tears streaming down their cheeks. No tears came from me. I was numb; I had no emotion, no connection to what this was.

I was accustomed to the presence of death. My grandfather used to take my sister and me to funerals all the time. He would leave us to our own devices to entertain ourselves while he visited. We would go up to the casket and check out the bodies of those who had passed, touching them with childhood innocence, examining what death was. They were not family to us and we rarely knew who they were. It wasn't an emotional experience – it was simply a matter of fact.

Grandpa knew everyone in town, and he checked the obituaries daily. We went to every funeral in our small town as a matter of course, without question. We lived next to the church – and across the street from the doctor – who lived next to the funeral home. At the end of the street was the old school which had been converted to a nursing home. That was life when I was growing up as a small child. Grandpa always insisted that Katelyn and I join him at all the funerals.

Grandpa would walk into the room as my sister and I were playing and ask, "Who wants to go for a ride?" More often than not that meant a ride to the nursing home, to a funeral, or off to visit a shut-in somewhere in the countryside. Shut-ins were people who, for any number of reasons, rarely or never left their home. My grandpa knew who they were, and he would always stop and visit, bringing fresh vegetables from the garden and some literature, as he called it. That was his way of witnessing, passing along bible-study material to those he didn't see at church each week. My sister was quick, and she knew that this question was a trick. She usually found a way out of the invitation with ease. I was always hopeful that the invitation might mean going to the dairy farm, or to visit an Amish family's home. As soon as I asked where we would be going on the ride, it was over – and I would have to go.

I didn't mind going to the nursing home. Grandpa would leave me in a room with one of the elderly women, and say he would be back soon. I would get tea and cookies and visit with them. Sometimes they would teach me how to do something, like crochet, or let me explore the trinkets they had in their small room. Sometimes Grandpa would come back and take me to another room and disappear again. When it was time to go he would come and get me, and we would go home.

If we went visiting at someone's house, he would introduce me and then tell me they had goats, chickens, peacocks – whatever it was that might be of interest –and then I was free to go. I could play with the animals by myself until it was time to leave. I loved animals, and I loved the freedom to be alone and explore outside. If it was a long visit, I would take off through the meadows and out to the woods by myself for hours.

Grandpa said people needed comforting in times of suffering, and the presence of children was important. I was taught that at the worst of times, in the darkness, the voices and laughter of children, of innocence, must be heard and remembered. At those times, people desperately needed a sign of hope, a reminder of the possibility of a future, the promise of better days. He would say that people needed to let go of the suffering they were experiencing and move on as quickly as possible. To grieve was okay, but you didn't stay there. That would be like saying that God didn't know what was best. To him, grieving outwardly was a sign of a lack of faith in God's Divine plan.

This was all new to me, being in a hospital and experiencing the death of a loved one. I had witnessed death so many times that I thought I understood what to expect. Witnessing death is without emotion – while experiencing death is to feel the loss, separation and confusion throughout your entire being. Where I grew up as a small child, there were no hospitals. I had never been to a hospital until my dad got a job at a hospital, forcing us to leave the country behind. I was never sick until we left the country. My only visit to a real hospital wasn't until I was almost twelve years old.

I left the hallway and the nurses, and walked back to the waiting room. Everyone had heard the news. I smiled and comforted those nearby. I reached out to the remaining families, waiting for their own loved ones to recover in the ICU. I did my best to be kind and supportive to them, to encourage them and tell them that their loved ones would be okay – that they would get better and return home with them soon.

I said goodbye to Marcos' friends and family. I got Felipe's car seat and stroller, put them together and walked away. My behavior was the normal behavior of someone leaving a social gathering with friends and family. I gave my well wishes and words of support, collected my things and got ready to leave. I didn't know any other way to react, to behave. I had never lost someone close to me. I had been in the presence of death many times, but it had never touched me personally before this moment.

I was almost to the elevator when Marcos' Uncle Rudy caught me. He said he had stayed behind in the room with Marcos, and that Marcos' head had swelled tremendously in a very short time. He made a large circle in front of his face with both hands, to show me its size, saying, "You should consider not having an open casket." I said, "I just saw him – he's fine, he looked at peace, like there had never been an accident. I'm sure we can have an open casket." I thanked him for letting me know and stepped back into the elevator, watching him as the doors closed.

My strength was slipping, now that the doors had closed and I was leaving it all behind. My strength had been based on a belief, a hope, that all would return to normal. I stepped out of the elevator on a random floor, and struggled to find my way out of the hospital. All my strength had been focused on an effort to survive. I no longer had a purpose. I had survived – now what was I supposed to do?

I couldn't keep my bearings. In the course of a few hours, my life had changed forever. I kept swinging between being confident, standing up and being in my power – to being completely lost and broken. I would be resolute, clear, moving forward one moment; then slip back into fear, isolation and a raw state of survival. I couldn't hold on much longer. I was shattering – my transformation was in mid-stride – phasing between who I had been and who I was becoming.

Chapter 4

Back Home

I made it home after driving aimlessly, deliriously banging through the parking lot and on through the dark streets of the night, back to where it had all begun. Back to where I had been lying on the couch, watching Felipe sleep soundly in his car seat. My mind went blank. I left my body to follow through, as my soul checked out. I got Felipe out of the car seat, found my way to the bedroom, placed Felipe into the bassinet next to my bed – the actions of my body alone.

Katelyn told me I had to get some sleep. Luna might have been in the house, I'm not sure. I didn't know who was there. I remember Katelyn; I focused on her. She told me again to go to bed. I lay down, cold, freezing, my body shaking uncontrollably. I couldn't get warm; there was no heat generating within me. It was as if the life force had left my body. I looked over to the bassinet and saw Felipe asleep, resting without a concern.

I couldn't sleep. My mind was alert and in a state of alarm. In the car, my adrenaline had begun pumping, trying to get me conscious enough to find my way home. Now I was alert, unable to shut off the energy I had called forth for that last bit of strength I needed to get home. I rolled over and talked to Marcos, as if he continued to lie beside me in his usual spot. I could feel his presence in bed with me. His presence wasn't in the hospital as the machines were turned off. Instead, he was here now.

I told Marcos how confused and scared I was – how I didn't understand what was happening or why. Why didn't he come home? Why didn't he get better? Why didn't he fight as he always had? I didn't understand why this was happening, why he had left Felipe and me. He'd always had the strength to decide, to declare the outcome and overcome any obstacles. Why had he chosen to leave us behind? I knew he was here with me; why didn't he answer? Why had hope let me down? I believed in the signs. I had placed faith, trust in my devotion, in a power greater than my own – why wasn't that enough? Acceptance and understanding eluded my grasp.

Katelyn returned to check on me. She knew my nervous cough. I had begun coughing uncontrollably. I couldn't make it stop. I was gagging, and my body was dry-heaving, as there was no food in my stomach to throw up. She wanted me to eat something. People had brought all sorts of food to the house while I was at the hospital. I couldn't eat. I continued coughing without end. I was choking, hollow and empty; there was nothing left within me to release.

This was what I had done since childhood. When I would get nervous or afraid, I would cough. I coughed, until I was gagging, dry-heaving or throwing up. I would get so upset I couldn't gain control of myself. Katelyn calmed me down, with her commanding presence, saying, "You do not have the luxury of this right now. Lie down and get some rest. We have a lot to take care of tomorrow." Felipe was still sound asleep next to me. Not a cry came from him. He was protected by an unseen presence through it all. I dozed off, and fell into a deep sleep.

The morning came, and people began arriving. I didn't want to put Felipe down. I didn't want anyone else to hold him. We only had each other. We made each other feel safe. We couldn't be apart. I didn't want to be with other people. I didn't want to talk. I wanted to be alone. I couldn't eat. They tried to make me. I couldn't allow anything in, not even water. I was a shell, empty and void.

Powerless

There was nothing I could do. I couldn't get away or make it all stop. There were decisions to be made. It was nearly Easter when Marcos passed on April 2, 1996. The Catholic church was not available for funerals. Marcos' Aunt Lindy had been working to make arrangements. She needed to know if I wanted to wait until the church was available to have the funeral, or have the services at Lujan's Funeral home in Taos. I wasn't Catholic and didn't want to prolong the mourning of Marcos' death. The church being closed for funerals during Easter week wasn't a custom I was familiar with. I was raised Baptist. Marcos was no longer a practicing Catholic. He preferred non-denominational Christian churches to Catholicism.

    I chose instead for the funeral to be held at Lujan's Funeral Home. Aunt Lindy made arrangements to have Marcos' body driven from Albuquerque to Taos. I was relieved to not have the funeral in the Catholic church. I didn't know their rituals; kneeling, standing, crossing themselves, receiving communion from the priest. I was already lost and struggling to get my bearings; having a Catholic service wouldn't make things any better.

    My choice meant that Luna would not be able to have the rituals and ceremonies important to her culture and beliefs. She was a woman of great faith, and she believed strongly in how a Catholic should pass into death and be buried. I was not able to extend this sort of compassion and sympathy when she needed it. I believed I was doing what Marcos would have wanted; that was all I wanted, to fulfill his wishes. I was gaining my power and didn't fully understand the consequences of my choices. I didn't want to hold my voice any longer. I struggled to regain power over a life that was completely shattered, out of control. This was not who I had been. This was not the life I had been living.

I had been living in New York City on summer break from art school, attending SUNY Purchase, when I had a dream that I would be in New Mexico in an adobe home with a baby in my arms. When I woke up, the morning after the dream, I went to the New York Public Library to look for colleges in New Mexico. There were two listed, the University of New Mexico and New Mexico State. I picked the University, which was in Albuquerque. I had heard of Albuquerque from cartoons as a kid, and it wasn't as close to Mexico. All I had heard of Mexico was bad – abductions of women, drugs, and violent crime. I applied to college in New Mexico and never returned for the fall semester of my third year at SUNY Purchase. I left New York City, went back to upstate New York and worked at the local hospital, missing the fall semester, until I got accepted into UNM, contingent upon a review of my work by the dean.

I drove to New Mexico with all my belongings in my grandpa's car with him behind the wheel. I had never been further west than Ohio. My grandpa insisted I not drive alone across the country. We had a great time staying in the cheapest motels. He paid nineteen bucks for a room with bloodstains on the sheets and cinderblock walls. I thought it was hilarious; this was him protecting me. Grandpa was raised during the Depression, and he was always frugal to a fault.

He once had my mom drive with a plastic yogurt container all the way to SUNY Purchase, an eight-hour drive, filled with peaches that had the bad spots cut out – along with a trunk full of acorn squash. My roommates thought I must be the poorest kid they ever met. I laughed – the peaches were delicious. They are at their sweetest when they are so ripe that they fall to the ground. Bruised from the fall, they have brown spots. Cut out the bruise and you have delicious, perfectly ripe fruit.

When I came to New Mexico I was a strong, confident artist, not afraid to pick up and move halfway across the country. No family or friends to support me; ready to begin a new life on my own. Grandpa cried as he drove away, leaving me standing in front of the dorm rooms. As he pulled away, in a breaking voice he said, "You won't be a local girl anymore." That was it – I never returned to New York to live again.

How did I go from the confident, strong, free, healthy girl I had been, eating organic fresh foods picked by my own hands, to this fat, unhealthy woman with no confidence – lost and unable to move forward? I ate what I was given, without question or resistance. I ate greasy foods and take-out, food bought in bulk from Sam's Club, food fried in oil and loaded with fat. Gone were the fresh-picked raw fruits and vegetables.

Lost was the free little girl within me. The girl whose backyard was her domain, surrounded by everything she loved. Then, I ran in the woods, talked with the animals and laughed with the flowers. Now I sat in the house all day, sinking into the couch, looking out the window at the sun shining without me. The happy days of clear skies and bright light seemed dim, even in memory.

Chapter 5

The First Date

I began to reflect back at how I arrived at this moment, as I remembered our first date. I was a walk-in at the hair salon where Marcos worked. The safety of the salon, the professional environment and his buoyant personality all encouraged me to be spontaneous, and say yes, without considering. I gave him my number in the parking lot, as he raced out the door to catch me before I pulled away. I consented to a first date in his home town of Taos. I had no idea at the time that it was a three-hour drive from Albuquerque.

I was nervous, anxious, when he pulled up to my apartment. A raccoon tail was hanging from the rear-view mirror of his white Camaro. I was unsure of myself as I climbed into the car. I had waited until he arrived to check my internal compass, to weigh if this was the right choice to go on an impulse date out of town with someone I had just met. He appeared so different outside of the salon, dangerous and unknown. I hesitated, if only in my mind – was it okay to get into the car with this man I barely knew?

On the road, Marcos was aggressive and angry. He was speeding, challenging other drivers and racing to get ahead. The dashboard cover was made of a green, carpet-like material, embroidered in red letters that read, "Jesus Is Lord," in front of the passenger seat. He had a custom license plate that read something along those same lines. I knew I should feel safe, reassured that he was openly religious, but I was terrified instead. His actions and outward appearance didn't match his messaging.

Marcos was a wild animal at the wheel, and he looked like a gang member. He had three gold teeth: one front tooth and two on the side in a row. He dressed like a Harley guy and had tattoos. I had only known him for the length of time it took to trim my long, straight hair. My fear, self-doubt and lack of confidence in myself to make the right choices all began to eat at my thoughts.

I was taught not to judge people by appearances. I was trying to be the good girl and believe the best of everyone. I didn't say no to getting in the car and going to Taos with him that day. I didn't honor my instinct and intuition that warned me that this may not be safe, and that this man might not have my best interests at heart. I went along, as if I had no choice, following the hands of fate.

Here I was, now, with Marcos dead, and I was questioning the hands of fate. Was this what all of the decisions I had made on that fateful first date had led me to? My complete inability to say no, to stand up for myself or trust my intuition, had all led me here. I had lost myself completely. I had been nearly erased, as I had accepted his leadership without question. Was this the part of me that had been released, as I laid my hand upon Marcos in the emergency room?

The day I went to the salon was a treat. I had been recovering from an illness, a urinary tract infection that had gone untreated. It mutated into a kidney infection that turned critical, as my blood became poisoned by the rampant infection within my body. I was completely broken, homebound for a month, as my body healed and repaired itself. I was weak, vulnerable, walking gingerly, having lost a great deal of weight in the process of recovery.

My roommate wanted to get me out of the house and back into life. She took me with her to get her hair done. She had an appointment and said I could go as a walk-in, and that it would be fine. Until then I had been isolated, reading and healing my body for weeks. I had never gone to a nice hair salon before, so I said yes, and I tagged along.

Reflecting back to that day, perhaps I said yes to that first date because I felt I was too weak to say no, or I believed I needed a protector at the time. My body was vulnerable. I had been alone for days on end, with my roommate attending classes at the university while I was too sick to go myself. It was all a part of what had to come to deliver me to this moment. If I believed there were no mistakes, no coincidences, then this was meant to be.

Our first date to Taos was to be a day trip, but we spent the night at his mother's house instead. We slept on a couch in the living room. She didn't want him to leave after coming for an afternoon visit, as it was a three-hour drive back to Albuquerque. I was stunned – this was not the plan. I didn't want to be rude to anyone, his mother in particular, so I conceded to their plan. I called my roommate to notify her that I would not be returning that night. I could hear the concern in her voice. This was not acceptable behavior, or an appropriate request, for a first date. She had clear boundaries for herself, learned and taught from childhood.

My reflection showed me that from the beginning I had not voiced my needs, opinions or concerns. I was more worried about not being rude. I had placed the desires of others above my own needs for comfort and security. I had played the victim, feeling that it didn't matter if I was uncomfortable. It didn't matter that I felt it was an inappropriate request. Luna and Marcos were excited; they had so much they wanted to do. I was a third wheel.

I blamed them for not being responsible for how I felt. Marcos should have said no, and made the three-hour drive back to Albuquerque, as planned, as promised. I didn't feel I could make the request and create an inconvenience. I should have said no. It was my responsibility to myself to speak up, but I stayed silent. No power, no voice emerged.

Marcos wanted me to see everything, meet everyone. It was as if we had planned this trip for months, years. Not an impulse date, set at a hair salon for a walk-in appointment, with a stylist I had never met. The hand of fate seemed to be pushing me, speeding me on the journey to this moment of transformation, sitting in the waiting room. I moved in with Marcos a few months after our first date.

It was as if I had never reflected on my own life until now. I was a stranger to myself, as though I had been seeing life through someone else's eyes. The strength growing within me was changing how I perceived everything. I realized that I had begun surrendering my power, the control over my own life, since our very first date. Marcos had begun taking authority over my decisions, one choice at a time. I let Marcos decide everything. He was adamant that his choices were for the best. I didn't resist or fight to voice my opinion, so he took what he wanted.

I figured I wasn't bringing much to the table. I wasn't from a wealthy family, my work-study job didn't pay much, I lived on nothing before I met him. I didn't own a car; I had to walk everywhere I went unless my roommate could give me a ride. I hated to ask, so I walked most of the time. Everything I experienced with him was new, and most of it was something I couldn't afford on my own.

He would let me borrow his car to run errands while he was at work. All he asked was that I pick him up from work at the end of the day. I didn't stop to consider that this ensured I would see him every day – or that I would end up staying the night if I borrowed his car, as he wouldn't feel like driving me home after work and dinner.

I was terrified to drive the Camaro. It would lunge to a start, like a shot from a gun, as the light turned green. It would hydroplane when it rained – momentarily lifting above the sidewalk – returning, I don't know how, to the road. The gas cap had a keyed lock I could never open, and I would have to ask strangers at the gas pump to help me unlock it each time I needed gas.

When I was a teenager I used to drive an old, rusty red, four-wheel-drive flatbed truck, with wooden slats for side rails. I had tires thrown in the back to provide weight when it snowed, to keep the back end from spinning out. When I got stuck in the snow, I would have to get out and manually turn the hubs on the front wheels to engage the four-wheel drive. A Camaro was not something I was used to. We were opposites, two distinctly different people and cultures, colliding in laughter and submission. He was naturally dominant and I was conditioned to be submissive, to seek approval, to gain love and acceptance.

I moved into his apartment, filled with his things, a few months after our first date. It was easier this way, as I was staying there most nights anyway. I was happy not to be sleeping in the living room of the apartment I shared with my roommate. She and I had lived in a one-bedroom apartment – she had the bedroom and I had the living room. When I moved in with Marcos, he asked me to throw away a lot of my things. The pig skull I had salvaged and cleaned from an old bar-b-que in high school. The dead butterflies and bugs I had collected and treasured over the years – these had to go too. Though I used my collectibles for drawings and paintings in my art classes, he said that since they were dead, it was sacrilegious to have them in the home. I argued at first, but he was adamant.

He was a pack rat – every surface and drawer was filled with his things. There was no room for anything of mine. He bought a dresser so I would have a place to put my clothes. I had the space on top of the dresser for my personal belongings. He had his own dresser, and a full closet, before I came. He bought me new clothes that he liked to see me wear. I hated them, and pushed them to the back of my dresser drawers. Low-cut velvet tops covered in flowers – and tight girl jeans – was not my style. He laughed at the clothes I already had – baggy pants and oversized tops. He worried over how skinny I was. He said it wasn't healthy.

Everything about me changed when I moved in with Marcos, except for my clothes. The oversized fishing jacket was staying; the skin-tight velvet flower shirts and girl jeans he bought were not. That was the one thing I would not relinquish my power over. My clothes were my protection, my way of hiding in plain sight. They provided security and confidence when it was lacking within. Marcos was constantly taking on new identities in his clothes, from zoot suits to Harley gear. He could be anyone he wanted; he exuded confidence and had his own personal style. I loved that about him.

All the food we bought, the meals made and the restaurants where we ate, were tailored to meet his appetite. I had been eating canned corn when I was living with my roommate; I didn't say no to any food. New Mexico was new to me, so I didn't care where we went to eat. I could never afford to eat out on my pay anyway. For the most part, I went along with all of his decisions, except for brief moments when I would get frustrated while riding in a car and not knowing where I was going. I would ask where we were going, saying I was bored or tired, only to hear it didn't matter if I knew – just enjoy the ride. It pushed my buttons, reminding me of riding with Grandpa as a child, but I figured it wasn't my car, so I didn't really have a say anyway.

I didn't understand the bigger picture of what was happening, that my control, my choices and my personal power were being taken from me. I figured that Marcos knew more and was more experienced, and that I could trust him to know what was best. I gave him power over everything. I was happy, if he was happy. It was an adventure seen and experienced through his eyes. I hardly even noticed that I no longer existed beyond being a passenger in his life.

Marcos adored me, and he was extremely protective, even jealous. I felt safe and cared for in his presence. He bought me a cell phone to keep with me in case I needed him. I was the first person in my family to own a cell phone. He would pick me up from my night classes at the University, and he would give me the keys to his white Camaro while he was at work. These were the signs that I was loved, that he had my best interest at heart.

Engaged

I brought Marcos home with me at Christmas to meet my family and to share with him the home I lived in during my teenage years. My family loved him immediately. He had a sweet, extravagant, flamboyant personality. He was kind, funny and warm, like a child exploring how different our worlds were from one another's. We told my family at Christmas of our plans to marry. He had actually asked me to marry him on our first date, while we slept smashed together on his mom's couch. I had thought he was joking and said yes, only to realize the next day that he was serious. From that first date on, he never wavered in his desire to marry me.

My mom brought us to her jeweler, and we picked out an antique ring for our engagement: an old platinum ring, with a center diamond flanked by two oval diamonds on the side. The jeweler rode Harleys himself, and he liked Marcos. They connected immediately on a very deep level. He designed and created a special ring for Marcos with a small cross engraved in the center.

The only problem in our relationship was that Marcos needed to be in control of all aspects of our life, for my own good and well-being, in his opinion. I accepted this without considering what I was giving up. He took the lead without hesitation, never questioning his own authority. He believed he was right, knew best and should have the final word. He didn't do this in an angry way. He just did it knowing he could, and that his will would be heeded. It was more like a parent-child relationship than equal partners about to be married. He was my self-appointed protector.

I traded my power for protection, not realizing that I already had all the power I needed to protect myself. I gave away my control without question – trusting that I would be cared for – and that all my needs would be met, all my desires realized. I relinquished all power, with only minor resentment, when my voice was completely denied, my opinion relegated to the nether regions of consideration. It was my choice to accept his behavior. He promised to protect me and I accepted the terms of his protection. He told me how much he cared for me as he made choices that benefitted him, unconcerned as to how they affected me. When we visited his mom in Taos, and I would ask to leave, saying I needed to get back to Albuquerque to finish my assignments for the next day – like a child asking permission of a parent – the answer would always be no. We would leave when he was ready. We moved on his time frame, his schedule. I never fought back. I gave in and waited, watching the clock, anxious for how long I would have to wait – and not knowing how long that would be.

Marcos voiced what he liked in my paintings, and he dictated what he thought I should paint. He never questioned his opinion or authority to advise me. He projected his personal power and voice in all matters. He was confident, self-assured and committed to his way of thinking and believing. His favorite topics and opinions revolved around religion. He preferred religious iconography in my paintings; his family and culture had painted images of Catholicism for generations.

It was a religion that was not my own. I was raised Protestant, a Baptist. My grandfather was a deacon in the church. Marcos and my grandpa were the same in many ways. Grandpa always stated what he thought was best, and if you didn't do as he instructed, his judgment was overwhelming. He was relentless in his adherence to structure, rules and a pious life, just as Marcos was.

Marcos told me where we would live, and what I would do for a career. It was all part of his master plan to be back in Taos, living in a newly renovated addition to his mother's home. He would open a hair salon, selling Aveda products. I would have a gallery in the salon and sell my paintings. I agreed with everything. He had a plan, so I didn't have to. He took control and commanded authority. I was used to being treated this way. Besides, I didn't have to work to create a dream – I just surrendered to *his* dream. I didn't have to take responsibility for creating a life of value – a life lived on purpose.

The Wedding

Our wedding was planned in every detail by Marcos and his mom. It was as if he were the bride; it was his special day. I felt that I was just present to agree, go along, without opinion. It was funny to see how excited he was about planning our wedding. I did set some boundaries, as his mom was planning to have giant bows hanging in the trees, and Marcos wanted to invite his former girlfriends. (Even his mom and aunts agreed that *that* was unacceptable!)

Marcos found the pattern for my wedding outfit, and he personally designed his own. We had our outfits made of suede, hand sewn by a friend of Marcos, a local Taos craftswoman. The silver buttons were handmade by another local artisan. No expense was spared in creating Marcos' vision of the perfect Harley-Davidson wedding.

I can remember the surprise of his co-workers. They couldn't believe I would consent to all that he was planning, which made me laugh even more. I couldn't see that that they were shocked by how inappropriate they felt his behavior was. A wedding was supposed to be a shared dream – not the dream of one person only. Marcos even bought a brand-new Harley-Davidson. A black Road King motorcycle for our honeymoon, so we could drive the bike through the mountain passes of Colorado in May. That wasn't my idea of a honeymoon. I had never ridden on a motorcycle for any length of time, and I absolutely hated being cold. Colorado in May is cold, and the mountains are usually still covered in snow.

My family all came for the wedding. My mom and her boyfriend Guy, my dad and his new wife Sharon, Katelyn my older sister, and Joseph my younger brother. Grammie and Grandpa, Uncle Viktor and Aunt Lily, all were there. Except for Viktor and Lily's three kids, this was my entire family. No one had visited New Mexico before, except for my mom and dad, who had honeymooned in Santa Fe decades earlier.

Our wedding was held in Luna's orchard, in the backyard of her family home. This was where Marcos envisioned us raising a family. It was May of 1995, nine months after our first date. Every detail was choreographed by Marcos and Luna, down to the flamenco dancers on wood platforms and large puppet statues called Gigantes, placed at random in the orchard on fruit-picking stands. Luna had made the Gigantes by hand with her brother in the traditional Spanish tradition. They were used in the Taos fiesta parade every year, with volunteers acting out the parts while wearing the giant puppets over their heads and bodies.

It was a traditional Northern New Mexico wedding in every way, including the Harley theme. Guests arrived wearing jeans, Harley shirts and dresses of all varieties. One guest even wore a knife tied to his belt. I heard many chuckled responses from my family. To say it was a culture shock for them would be an understatement. They loved every minute; it was a true spectacle for them.

An uncle on Marcos' father's side, who raised goats and sheep, agreed to butcher two goats and a lamb for the wedding reception. The meat was cut, wrapped in foil and placed in two large pits that had been dug in the ground. The meat was then covered with hot stones heated in a nearby fire. The earth was shoveled back on top of the hot stones and left to cook through the night. It was an old tradition passed down for generations, and hungrily anticipated by those who remembered eating it in the past.

There were red and green chile stews by the five-gallon bucket, which a local restaurant owner and friend gave Marcos for the reception. We had twenty chocolate cakes made by his Uncle Carl. The cakes were all chocolate, with chocolate frosting, as Marcos had wanted. Not a single white cake among them to signify the typical wedding cake. They were shaped in hearts and crosses, decorated with white, frilly icing. We had so many cakes that guests were leaving with their own cakes to take home.

As the bride, I had most of the expenses charged to my credit card, to be paid by my work-study job at the University of New Mexico. I made $4.50 an hour, working part time. I was a full-time student finishing my degree in Fine Arts. I was left with a bill that took months to pay off. Many of the guests contributed, bringing food and other items to help ease the burden. I greatly appreciated the help. I was also still making payments to the jeweler back in New York to pay for Marcos' custom-designed ring.

The Honeymoon

After the wedding, Marcos and I drove the Harley to a bed-and-breakfast at the base of the mountains at the Taos Ski Valley. It was dusk as we arrived. We went straight to bed and fell asleep. We were exhausted. I was already pregnant, three months along, by the time we were married. No pregnancy test had been done, but that didn't make it not so. My wedding outfit had to be let out to make room for my expanding body. Marcos didn't want anyone to know; he was in denial. No mention was to be made of my belief or feelings that I was pregnant. I had told no one, not even my mom, that I was pregnant.

I believe Marcos was afraid of what people would think, that they would know he wasn't the perfect Christian if I was pregnant. He also expressed concern that his insurance wouldn't cover the pregnancy, if it happened before we were married. We waited until after the honeymoon to go to an OBGYN and get a pregnancy test. The doctor was frustrated and upset with me for not getting a pregnancy test sooner, and for not taking the appropriate steps to protect my unborn child. She could not comprehend our level of ignorance. She said that the first three months of pregnancy were crucial for the development of the fetus. I had no idea. I had never talked about having kids, and I wasn't allowed to tell anyone, including my mom, so no one could tell me that what I was doing was foolish or dangerous.

The doctor looked in judgment and disdain at Marcos and me as we sat before her. I didn't say a word. I had wanted to take a pregnancy test when I first suspected, but Marcos said no. After the first two months I knew I was pregnant. Marcos didn't agree, but I knew I was right. He was still in denial. He had said it wasn't possible for him to get me pregnant, and I believed him, so I never took any measures to protect myself.

I was exhausted throughout our honeymoon. We drove up to Colorado on the motorcycle, touring from town to town. We followed the back roads and long, twisting mountain passes. We stayed in dive hotels to save money, eating at cheap diners. I was freezing all the time. It was cold, wet and rainy for almost the entire trip. In some places there was snow on the ground, just as I had suspected. We came back into New Mexico in time for all the Memorial Day Harley rides. Marcos, of course, had wanted to coordinate our honeymoon with the events.

I was so bundled up on the back of the motorcycle that you couldn't even see my face. I would pass out within minutes each time we started driving – knocked out cold on the back of the motorcycle. I couldn't help it. I was utterly drained, as my body tried to remain warm and nourish my baby growing within me. All I wanted was sleep. All of this was

Marcos' fantasy. I helped him fulfill his dreams without regard for my own needs or desires. I had no energy remaining to even dream of what I might want to create for my own life, and the life of my child to come. I had given up everything I wanted, so as to help Marcos follow his every whim. I loved Marcos very much. He was sweet, loving and kind – but there was nothing left of me. I smiled, laughed and listened to how his day had been. I had given up everything to live through his eyes. I was a shell; I could no longer remember my own hopes and dreams, if I'd ever even had any.

On the first night of our honeymoon trip in Colorado, Marcos made love to me. While making love, he made some comment about knocking to say hello to our son. I don't know why, but I was repulsed, turned off – it was as if I didn't exist. I had given up so much of myself already. This last piece taken, in our intimate moment, was the breaking point. I reflected back, looking at my old self compared to this moment, and I was repulsed by my own reflection. I felt like nothing more than a vessel to fulfill his wish to have a son. I didn't make love to him again for the rest of our honeymoon. I blamed the pregnancy, being tired and not feeling well. I never made love to Marcos again.

Felipe Born

Once we'd returned from our honeymoon, and after we'd met with the doctor to confirm my pregnancy, Marcos told everyone how excited he was to become a father. He would make plans for himself, our son and his mom in the future, and he would tell everyone what he thought was best for his unborn child. He would daydream of what adventures he and his son would go on together. I would get jealous and mad. Filled with self-pity, I would say, "Why don't you just marry your mother? You don't need me. I'm just the vessel to deliver the baby for you both."

Luna and Marcos had dreamed of doing so many projects together. Marcos was going to move back to Taos, start a salon and live on the other half of their 100-year-old adobe family home. Luna had planned for Marcos to take care of her as she aged; he was the executor of her will. They had a shared bank account already in place. Everything had been planned without me, long before I had arrived for that first date. I had no voice, no power, no control over my own destiny. I was the facilitator of a small portion of their dream, nothing more.

I knew Marcos loved me dearly, and that this was a part of his culture, upbringing and age. He was ten years my senior, from a small mountain town in Northern New Mexico. This was a way for him to experience childhood with his mother. He had been raised in many ways by Mama Mercy, his mother's mother. This was their chance to live out the child-parent relationship they had missed. I was a willing participant for the most part. It was my choice to live another person's dream – watching another person's life unfold – separate, as it was, from myself. I didn't fight for myself; I didn't stand up and make my opinions, thoughts and plans known. I didn't create my own life. I submitted to Marcos and his life.

It was his choice to control me, to use his power and innate authority, to maintain my obedience and devotion. He didn't trust that I would love him without his control. I had always thought that he was so strong and confident. In truth, he was profoundly insecure, with a young and attractive wife. He was afraid he would lose me at any moment. That was another reason for his hasty proposal, and insistence on a wedding, before we had even known each other for a year.

I was still attending the university, surrounded by people my own age. Marcos was never suited for college. He had tried it when he was younger, and quickly dropped out to pursue his own freedoms. I believe he was threatened by my independence during the day, fearful that I would meet someone else. That was part of the reason he gave me a cell phone, so he could be aware of where I was and what I was doing at any moment.

I struggled, during my pregnancy, with both my health and the stress of my work load. I had continued with a full course of study at the university, and I maintained my work-study job, as I had before the wedding. I had bills to pay and school to finish. Adding to that, I began to experience extreme lightheadedness to the point of fainting. If I stood still for any length of time, I feared I would pass out. When I stood, I would begin to sweat profusely, followed by seeing stars in my vision. That would escalate to a loss of hearing – and then I would be out. If I could sit down and get something to eat, my blood sugar would rise and I would be fine. But for some reason, standing still would trigger the episode. I would be shopping at the grocery store, and head to the checkout with all of my items – and I'd have to leave them in the cart if there was a line. I couldn't make it through the line to purchase my food. I would arrive back at home, saying I couldn't get what I needed to make dinner.

I was diagnosed with preeclampsia at the end of my pregnancy. My blood pressure would skyrocket, leaving the nurses threatening me with hospitalization. I would promise to bring it down – so I'd focus, rest for a moment and ask to be retested. My blood pressure would always drop enough to allow me to go home. I was barely 115 pounds before I became pregnant, and I had ballooned to 200-plus pounds by my ninth month. My body was a wreck – completely out of balance. I had no control over anything in my life.

I was eating all the foods that Marcos and his family typically ate. I was eating fried eggs that floated, as they cooked, in a pool of grease. I had milk, yogurt and dairy every day. Having grown up on raw milk, I learned that store-bought milk made me physically sick. Then there were all the times, while visiting Marcos' mom's house, that I would take a big gulp of milk, only to find that it had spoiled, leaving chunks of soured milk in my mouth. I was not active; I never went for walks or out for hikes. I was confined to the house for my own safety, except for going to the university to attend classes and to my work-study job.

I had lost my physical health, and I struggled to maintain my sanity, as the days trickled past my due date. Felipe was supposed to be a Christmas baby. But Christmas came and went with no signs of an impending birth. Friends and family continued to call, asking if we had good news. I finally stopped answering the phone. It drove me crazy to hear their questions, well wishes and excitement for an event that hadn't happened.

My delivery was difficult. Felipe was facing up; he had to do a backbend to come out, instead of rolling like a somersault. His head would start to come out, crown, then go back in. This happened again and again. I went deep within my own mind, closed my eyes and drew from my own inner strength. I would push, struggling to hold the force against Felipe's body being in the wrong position – and then his head would crown and go back in. I was so out of shape from having been sedentary for nine months and gaining close to ninety pounds. I no longer had the physical strength and endurance I needed so desperately at this time.

This struggle went on for hours, until daylight, with no pain medicine. I was never comfortable with drugs, and the procedure for the epidural scared me. I had never been admitted to a hospital for anything in my life. I was completely out of my element. I was giving birth to my first child, in the wrong position, without pain medicine, in a place where I didn't feel safe. I had asked for a home delivery and was told it wasn't allowed for the first child. I was openly lied to – and I had no idea.

Felipe was in distress; his heartbeat was accelerating and becoming erratic. The stress of trying to find his way out of the birth canal without success had caused him to have a bowel movement. The nurses were in a state of alarm. They had to deliver him now. There would be complications if he got the meconium in his lungs. If I couldn't push him out, they would have to prepare me for a caesarian. I went deeper within, my eyes closed to the world around me. It was too much to bear. This was not what I wanted. Every aspect of my life was out of my control.

Marcos was in a panic. I could hear him sitting in the chair by the door, praying out loud to God to intervene. He had begun speaking in tongues. I'd had no experience with that sort of thing before Marcos. The only other time I had seen him do it was when we were eating in a restaurant, and an elderly woman began choking. Marcos began praying and then speaking in tongues. He didn't reach out to the woman or her family. He just began praying like that in front of everyone. He got the same response now as he did then – everybody looked, and no one said a word. It was uncomfortable for everyone present to witness such unfamiliar practices in a moment of stress and alarm. All I knew was that I couldn't understand a word he was saying – and that it was freaking everybody out.

My eyes still closed, I could hear the nurses' shift change. A new midwife was in charge. There was urgency in her voice as she commanded that the baby had to come out now. I had to deliver him, or she would make the call for a caesarian. I pulled from deep within my being. I pushed with all my strength, ripping my insides apart. My body was giving way for my baby to come out, tearing my flesh, moving my organs to make way for what I was forcing to happen. I would protect my son. He would be safe. I wouldn't let him struggle in fear. He had to come out now, and I would get him here safely. My body was numb – the adrenaline had kicked in – it raised me above the unbearable pain. My son was born. I had delivered him.

The nurses rushed him away to clear the meconium from his nose and throat, to keep his lungs free, and to clean him up. Once they were certain he was fine, that he was in no danger, they laid him on my chest. I was so happy to see my baby, to hold him in my arms. I began nursing him right away. He was beautiful and perfect. The nurses told me after the delivery that my placenta was so thin and small that they were amazed he was born healthy. He was barely getting the nutrients he needed, going so far past his due date.

I spent the night in the hospital alone. They kept Felipe in the nursery with all the other babies, only bringing him to me when they felt he needed to nurse. I was bleeding heavily, and I could not walk without extreme difficulty and pain. I had been torn apart; sacrificed my body to free my son. The nurses told me that things should move back into place and the pain should go away soon. I could barely sit down – and each time I tried, I had to prepare myself for the rush of pain that would surge up my body.

I had picked clothes from my early pregnancy days to wear home after the birth. I wasn't prepared. I had no idea. I had barely lost ten pounds. My body was unchanged. I still looked nine months pregnant. I was in shock. My body riddled in pain, I had to wear the same clothes going back home that I had worn to the hospital. I was forced to face the reality of what remained of me – a broken, overweight woman with no self-esteem or confidence. I was both overjoyed with the birth of my beautiful son and devastated by what I had become. I loved my little Felipe Marcos Valentine, but life wasn't what I thought it would be.

Marcos picked all the names for our new son from his family. I had wanted Joseph like my brother, but that was not to be. He chose all Hispanic names to show his culture, his family pride. My voice, my culture, my print upon my son was nonexistent. Felipe was the spitting image of Marcos, with no resemblance whatsoever to me. I was erased without a trace. I was used up, and I had nothing left to give. I continued to try as best I could to be there for my son, struggling to survive.

Luna was not able to visit right away. She had taken off from work at Christmas, for the two weeks before Felipe was due, to be there for his delivery. He was late, and she was forced to go back to work. Marcos and I were alone together at the hospital to welcome him into the world. I was grateful for this privacy at the creation of our little family. Marcos' family came the next day, bringing food and gifts to celebrate. Life was moving forward, and we were happy as a family.

Felipe was beautiful, a perfect baby with a wonderful temperament. I was thankful and blessed to have him. My life was not my own, but that was fine, so long as I had my son. I felt safe, protected, with a lovely home and family. Everything was perfect, now that Felipe was here. We were moving forward. Marcos' old ways had softened into fatherhood. He was no longer a combative driver, fighting with those who would look in my direction. No one even looked anymore. He became gentle, calm, a cautious driver, a patient husband and a loving father.

In the week leading up to Marcos' accident, I had received a phone call from a friend I had grown up with in high school. She knew that I had married; we had lost touch until this call. I was telling her all about my new life – how perfect it was, and how happy I was with my new son and my marriage to Marcos. It was all true; I really was very happy. I felt like Shel Silverstein's depiction of the tree in *The Giving Tree*. I found a way to give more of myself each time there was a need. All I wanted was to create happiness for those I loved. In the end, though, there was nothing left of me to give. I was erased from existence.

Marcos had grown into a calm, loving and devoted husband, who looked after Felipe and me. All our needs were met. He would go to the grocery store and buy all the food, so I wouldn't have to leave the house and bring Felipe with me. He took the laundry to the laundromat and did hours of laundry at a time. He would wake up with Felipe in the early-morning hours and let me sleep, while he and Felipe would lie down in front of the TV and watch cartoons.

He would even make himself chocolate-chip pancakes, just as his mother had made them for him when he was a child. He would eat them as he and Felipe watched cartoons. He was sentimental about everything. To me, these were all signs of his knowing what was to come. He experienced every moment with his son and his family as precious.

Life was supposed to be moving forward. I was supposed to be healing, my body returning back to its pre-pregnancy state. My insides had been torn apart, but things had not shifted back as expected. I was still feeling excruciating pain when I had a bowel movement. I would cry out in pain, as if I were back in the delivery room all over again. I tried a laxative, which worked, but I would never know when it was going to kick in. I had no control over myself, my body, my emotions, or my life. I was a stranger in the mirror. I was enormous, in contrast to my usual small frame. My hair had been dyed from blond to reddish-brown. My long, wavy locks had been cut short in a layered pixie cut, a hormone-induced request I had made of Marcos one evening to change my looks entirely while I was pregnant.

I would spend the entire day alone in the house with Felipe. I was feeling lost and overweight, and suffering from bouts of post-partum depression. This would overwhelm me with sadness, regret and isolation. I would sit on the couch and feel it all, let the tears stream down my face and allow it to pass through me. I told no one; the guilt was too much to bear. How could I have such a beautiful son, a devoted and loving husband, and still be so depressed? In my eyes I had no control; no power to change anything I was experiencing in my life. I surrendered and allowed the emotions to flow freely. Sitting on the couch, I held Felipe in my arms and cried silently, looking out the window.

I was still suffering from undiagnosed post-partum depression when Marcos died. His death compounded the feelings of separation, isolation and hopelessness I was already experiencing. My hormones raging, my emotions swinging like a giant pendulum, I was a ship lost at sea. My North Star, my inner vision, had been lost, all navigation gone, all hope of finding home devastated with the loss of my focus upon the light within. I was a stranger to myself, adrift in a life I didn't recognize. I had not taken responsibility for my life, not made choices to live my life on purpose – creating value and meaning of my own choosing.

As I struggled with depression, Felipe became colicky in the evenings and would cry without end. It was emotionally exhausting for Marcos and me as new parents. We made it through by letting him swing until he felt better, or by holding him face-down on our laps. The homeopathic medicine we gave him took time to take effect. I tried to give him chamomile tea but he wouldn't drink it. Eventually I came to understand that I couldn't eat certain foods because Felipe was getting gas from my milk – as I was eating chile, beans, everything I had begun eating with Marcos. I researched, read about and taught myself what I needed to eat to help Felipe find relief. I did everything I could to care for my son. He was my life, my only reason for continuing to hold on.

Chapter 6

The Funeral

Standing before Marcos' body at the funeral home, I realized that Uncle Carl was right. He had stayed behind and watched as the swelling advanced at an alarming rate. He knew it was out of control, and that an open casket would be impossible. He had tried to prepare me, warn me of what was to come. I couldn't hear it at the time, as I was already firmly in the grip of shock, attempting to leave it all behind. I had to face it now, standing before Marcos. I couldn't let him be remembered this way.

I had requested that Marcos be buried in his wedding clothes. He was so proud of his custom-designed, black-leather outfit. He had handcrafted every detail to meet his ideal look and style. Luna thought it would be better to keep the wedding outfit, something to pass down to Felipe when he was of age. I didn't want to. Marcos had designed this for our wedding day. It was a reminder of our love for each other. It wasn't a symbol for Felipe – it was *our* symbol, the symbol of Marcos and me, committing to a life together – a life that turned out to have lasted less than one year. I wanted Marcos to be remembered as he had been on our wedding day – full of joy, pride and dreams for the future.

Marcos' wedding outfit included a custom black-leather hat with a white cross stitched on the front. It sat upon the top of his head, as he lay in the casket, like a small child's hat. His head had swollen to the size of a square pumpkin; his face nearly unrecognizable by the force of the swelling. I could feel that his soul was no longer present, no longer holding this form. His body was nothing more than an empty shell, cast aside. A thing to be discarded.

I still found myself talking to his old form, one more time, whispering to myself out loud. I spoke of what I saw, "Marcos, your head has swollen badly. I can't let your family and friends see you this way. You are so handsome, lying here in your wedding clothes, just as you were on our wedding day. I'm glad you will forever be as you were on that day. I can't pretend you are here any longer. This isn't you. I will find you in my heart. I know this is not you. You are not here, not in this body."

I stepped away, and the casket was closed. That old, worn and distorted form was not Marcos. I was directed to a seat at the front of the funeral home, and I waited. The room filled to overflowing, standing room only. His friends were standing in the lobby and outside the funeral home, showing their love and respect. Marcos was loved by many. He was generous, compassionate and fun to be with. His heart broke when the hearts of others broke. He was a beautiful soul in a rough exterior, a light in the darkness for those who had lost hope. He would remind them of his own journey, sharing his defeat and struggles with them. He would tell them of the forgiveness he had received and how his own life had been transformed.

The funeral service was different from any I had ever witnessed. Spanish and English were spoken. Strange men, part of a religious group who mourned the dead with Spanish songs, sat across the aisle from me. I couldn't understand the words of the songs they sang, or relate to the emotion of what they were singing. The songs sounded sad, filled with pain, sorrow and grief; the crying out of a tormented soul in anguish. My mind was left to create meaning from this pain that was expressed in falsetto.

Not connecting with the words outside of me, I went within. I felt joy welling within me, remembering Marcos, and how he believed that a funeral was a time of celebration. He would say, "I will be with my Lord. It is a time to rejoice." He had studied to be a pastor and had done missionary work around the world – in Mexico, Africa and New Zealand, among other countries. Death was a time of joy and celebration to him, based on a deep-seated belief in God and heaven.

He often spoke of such things, as his first fiancé had died in a car accident. She had fallen asleep at the wheel. Exhausted from his seminary training, and from driving back and forth from Albuquerque to Taos on the weekends, he had her drive back while he slept. She crashed the car and died beside him. Her daughter was asleep on Marcos' chest. The toddler had not been buckled or secured in a car seat. The little girl had flown out of the car and landed on the road, completely unharmed. His fiancé had died, and no one else had been injured.

Remembering Marcos, his strength and his joy, I stood up and told the story he would have wanted to share. The story of joy, of hope and overcoming. He wanted to share his story with everyone he met, that God had given him a second chance. He wanted everyone to know it was possible to change their ways; stop drinking, smoking and doing drugs, and live a new life. He believed it was never too late and that repentance had given him not only a new life but a loving wife and a beautiful son. A son he never thought possible for him to have.

I was happy sharing my joy that he was now in heaven. He believed adamantly in the afterlife, and that he would be in heaven after his death. I smiled and spoke of my love for him. I told everyone how I called him "Pea," short for "Sweet Pea." I shared how Marcos was prepared to die, as he had given his life to God. I repeated what I had heard him say on so many occasions. He was always sharing, witnessing, as my grandpa had. I would sit and listen. I knew his stories by heart.

I could see that people didn't understand. They thought I should be crying – heartbroken – unable to comprehend what was happening. That would come. This was not my moment. This was Marcos' moment. I would honor his wishes. I would stand up for him and let his voice be heard; make sure his message was shared with those he loved and who loved him in return. I would break, shattering in private, crying out to God while broken upon the floor, where no one could witness my suffering. This was not me. This was Marcos standing here. It was his attempt to comfort those who mourned the loss of his life.

Most of the people in attendance had just seen us on our wedding day, less than a year before. They couldn't even recognize me. I had gained weight, hacked off all my long, blonde hair and become a shell of a person. I was a completely different person than I had been at our wedding. Again, I assumed my newfound strength as I stood up and began speaking in front of everyone. I was no longer the quiet, shy girl standing behind, while Marcos did all the talking.

The Burial

When the funeral service ended, everyone scattered, as if being chased by an unseen terror. They had been packed into the funeral home, shoulder to shoulder, standing room only. I had been in the very front with the rest of the family, next to Marcos. All in attendance evacuated the building, racing to their cars, erupting from the parking lot like sparks from a fire. I was confused. What was happening? I gathered Felipe up and made my way slowly to the front doors of the funeral home.

I stepped out into the bright light of the sun, which felt soothing to my skin, as I held Felipe snugly in my arms. The new spring leaves shone on the trees bordering the parking lot. I watched, trying to make sense of what was happening before me. I had never seen anything like it. There was near panic, as families pushed their way into cars, desperate to get out of the parking lot ahead of the rest of the cars. I felt like I was witnessing the aftermath of a sporting event, or of July Fourth fireworks.

I was accustomed to people lingering to give hugs, say kind words of condolences, wanting to hold on to the moment a few seconds longer before saying goodbye. There was none of that; it was everyone for himself. A flurry of activity moving at record speed, racing to the unknown burial site in the distance. I couldn't understand – why was everyone in such a rush? Why was there such urgency to get to the burial site?

I didn't know where Marcos was to be buried. I didn't know where I needed to go next. I felt excluded from what was happening, from all the frenzy. I was merely a witness, an observer, trying to catch up with the scene unfolding before me. I was a foreigner, in a foreign land. Without Marcos as my guide and protector I was lost. I didn't know the dirt roads leading off in all directions. I didn't know what to expect next.

The funeral-procession cars, reserved for the family, were just beginning to pull away at the far end of the parking lot. I could hear people say that the family was leaving in the lead car that had just pulled out. I was afraid I would be left behind. I hadn't driven my own car. Remembering how lost I had been when leaving the hospital, I didn't want to be driving, once again not knowing where I was going. I began to panic. I had to get moving, jump into the frenzy and take the next opportunity I saw.

There was another limo not far from me. I didn't ask; I just climbed into the car and secured Felipe's car seat. Katelyn had found her way beside me. We made it; we joined the procession to the burial site. The driver knew where to go. I didn't ask any questions. I was relieved to have found an available car going to the next destination. As we pulled away, I scanned the parking lot for a familiar face, to no avail.

We took several twists and turns, winding down narrow dirt roads, passing familiar homes along the way. I was confused. We were headed past Luna's home and the rest of Marcos' childhood homes, away from town and through neighborhoods. I didn't remember ever seeing a graveyard near there. Why would we be headed away from Taos and out into the rural communities in the surrounding area?

    I could see cars parked up and down a narrow dirt road, lined with small adobe homes. This was it. Our driver was trying to find a place to park along the edge of the road. I could see people walking down the road, and up a small dirt pathway, into the back yard of one of the homes. The grasses were wild, with new shoots mixed with the old, dead growth from last year.

    I climbed out of the car and followed the procession down the road and back up the pathway. I watched my step as I carried Felipe, careful not to trip on the large stones that had fallen loose along the path with so many feet trampling to arrive at the burial site. Now I understood the urgency to leave the funeral home. Everyone knew there wouldn't be enough space to accommodate all who had come to mourn Marcos and see him buried. They were desperate to have a few final moments with him, to see him buried, secured into the Earth.

    I came into a small clearing, with stalls containing goats, and wild cats roaming in the center. I could smell the familiar scent of barnyard animals that I had grown accustomed to as a child. I could hear the throaty, cutting calls of the goats, distressed by the sudden intrusion of so many people. I caught glimpses of the cats racing to hide, kittens meowing for their mamas who had disappeared at the first sign of people.

I could see grave markers, crosses, plastic flowers and decorations of personal sentiment marking the memory of loved ones from long ago. The markers formed two clusters of graves, on either side of the stalls in the center. This was where they were putting Marcos' body – in this unmarked gravesite, hidden in a backyard I could never find on my own – and would never feel comfortable visiting again.

Generations of Marcos' family were buried here, in small plots dating back over one hundred years. Homes had been built around the gravesites, pressing upon the slumber of this ancient resting place. The goat stalls were added at a later date, I suspect, to accommodate the growing needs of the families nearby. Time had moved on; the graves remained. This was a place for children and animals to play now. Laughter amongst the dead, a constant reminder of the cycles of life and death.

His beloved Mama Mercy, Uncle Peto and other family members were buried here. His Aunt Lindy had given up a family plot she had purchased from the small co-op handling the affairs of the gravesite. She gave her plot for Marcos to be buried in her place. Burying children before their elders was not what anyone had planned.

I soaked up this moment – the stalls, the goats, the ancient grave markers. Dozens of people I didn't recognize crammed elbow to elbow, all a few feet off an old dirt road here in Talpa, New Mexico, surrounded by homes in the warm sunlight. Someone had come the day before and dug a deep hole in the earth to place the large, black coffin in its final resting place. A giant pile of dirt remained to one side of the hole. I found myself crammed closely between the edge of the pile of dirt and the hole in the ground, precariously balancing, before pressing myself back deeper into the crowd of mourners, away from the burial site.

I began coughing uncontrollably, as the moment became more real. The coughing turned to gagging and dry heaving, as usual. Marcos' ebony Laquerre casket, with his body inside, was about to be lowered within. I pressed myself further back, escaping to the safety of the goats. I couldn't witness this part. This was too real, too literal for me to bear. I was doubled over, trying to hold back the coughing. My only saving grace was that I hadn't eaten any food for days; there was nothing left to throw up. Not even bile escaped my body, only the horrible racking cough compressing my chest inward, bending me in half, producing nothing but fear and shame.

Katelyn and a friend of Marcos' ran to a neighbor's house to get me a glass of water to calm the coughing. I sipped slowly from the tall, clear glass, observing the homes of neighbors as they bore witness to Marcos' death. The goats and kittens cried out at the disturbance to their peace. The shock of this reality was chipping away at my stalwart exterior of cheer. I was thankful for the water, as I drank in this moment holding nothing back, falling apart completely. I forgot all the friends and family gathered nearby and allowed the goats and the kittens to comfort me. I was raw, vulnerable; exposed by my coughing and choking for breath as the frightened widow I had become.

It seemed wrong to put Marcos body in this place, to bury him with animals running around. I don't even know why it bothered me. I love animals, and Marcos without question would have wanted to be buried in this sacred space, reserved for members of his family and only a few others. It was the unexpected shock, the reminder, that I was a foreigner in a foreign land – without control, power or voice. That was the final straw that broke me. How would I ever find this place again? Marcos would be lost to me forever.

A few words were said, I presume. I couldn't hear over my coughing and recoiling in the distance. Before I knew it, we were leaving the gravesite. Marcos was buried and we were on our way back to Luna's house, in Ranchos de Taos, a few houses away from Talpa. Talpa was a small township containing no more than a few dozen homes.

Luna's sister Lindy lived next door to Luna, and up the hill was her father's house, Daddihijo, as Marcos had named him, where her brother Parker also lived. The house up the hill was Luna's family home, where she grew up with her seven brothers and sisters. Luna had inherited the old adobe home down the hill, where she now lived. It was her grandmother's before her, her father's mother, and was over one hundred years old.

My Family Arrived

I was so far removed from my body during the events immediately following Marcos' death that I barely realized my family had arrived, and that they were present for the funeral. I was disconnected, unaware of what was happening. They were there in that tiny backyard, as Marcos was lowered into the ground. I believed I was alone, isolated, forgotten. It was not true, as so many were there to support me. I couldn't see or accept their love; I was spiraling through time.

My mom came with her new husband, Michael. My dad and his wife Sharon had planned the trip in advance to celebrate Felipe's birth with Marcos and me. They already had their bags packed, and used their original tickets. The timing was just as they had planned it. The difference was that they had been coming to celebrate. Now their special trip was to be spent in mourning.

This was the first time anyone in my family was seeing Felipe. The celebration of life was now one of death, a single breath between moments. Marcos had been so excited for everyone to meet Felipe. His death brought us all together to share the moment Marcos had so much wanted to enjoy. It was as if everything was perfectly orchestrated, as all of Marcos' dreams came true in one small window of time – but the cost was too high to pay.

Marie, my childhood friend, arrived the night before and was staying with a friend of Marcos' family. Marie had come to visit, and meet Marcos, after he and I were married. Marcos absolutely adored Marie – her voice, how she left messages on the phone, her eccentric and intangible personality. He loved having her with us and welcomed her to visit anytime.

Like Marie, my family was spread out at different people's homes, except for my dad and Sharon who had a hotel room in town. They might have had one booked in advance, as they had already planned their visit. Everyone was cared for and treated like family. I was grateful to those who coordinated and made all of this happen, at a time when I was incapable of providing support.

My own experience of the funeral was so different. My family was feeling the embrace and warmth of a culture that loves and supports family. Marcos' family and friends would never allow family to stay in a hotel if they had accommodations available. Meals would be prepared, and every effort would be made to make them feel welcome, supported and fed. My experience of the funeral was one of isolation, of shutting out the love everyone wanted to share with me.

I was disconnected and on the defensive; everyone and everything was a threat to my existence. I had to hold on tight to Felipe for fear that someone would try to take him away from me. I barely let him out of my arms for more than a few moments. I was fully in survival mode. I didn't feel safe. I didn't trust the motivations or intentions of those closest to me.

I felt vulnerable without Marcos' ever-present protection. His presence was so dominant in my life that the void created by his absence made me paranoid. There was no one standing beside me, dictating what would happen when. Instead of feeling relief, I was terrified. I had depended on Marcos' telling me what to do in every situation. Now he was gone. I could still hear his words of instruction in my head from time to time, but that too was fading.

Reception Say No

After the burial, I returned to the safety of Luna's house. I didn't want to see anyone. I didn't want to hear any words of consolation or have anyone touch me. I didn't want to cry – I just wanted to be quiet. I wanted to escape from all of it to be in a place of safety. I wanted Felipe and me to be far away. I had to separate myself from all of this. My sister had always protected me; she was with me now, standing guard. She had no problem telling someone I wanted to be alone, and forbidding them access to me. We stayed at Luna's while everyone else went to Lindy's house next door for a reception. I couldn't do it anymore. I couldn't do any more obligations; no more crowds of people I didn't recognize. No more noise, no more situations I couldn't understand.

The emotional drain I experienced during this time was overwhelming. I lost over twenty pounds. I barely ate from the time of Marcos' accident until his funeral. I was nursing continually, and not sleeping through the night. When I did eat, it was the smallest nibbles I could keep down. I couldn't take this experience in. I couldn't accept what was happening; I was desperately trying to reject it all. Accepting it made it real. I couldn't allow that, not yet.

I had trouble finding black clothes that would fit for the funeral. I had found a pair of wide-leg black pants and a thin, gray sweater. That was the best I could do. My recent weight loss helped, but it was nothing compared to what I had gained during my pregnancy. I struggled to accept who I was; even in this moment I couldn't release the self-judgment and lack of self-esteem raging within me. I was being transformed, torn apart from the inside. All I wanted was permission to be – permission to hold this space for a time, to be alone without witness. My emotions vacillated between who I had been and who I was becoming. The old patterns and habits of being were fighting to keep hold of me, through the process of rebirthing.

Luna's house was where it had all started for Marcos and me, with our first date. My journey to this moment began here. Everything that came before, formed this moment. Marcos professed his love to me here. I surrendered my power here. My wedding took place here. It all happened so fast: first date, engaged, married, a new baby and widowed at record speed. I was floundering, trying to get my bearings and find my direction once again. I had no internal compass to guide me. I had dulled that voice within me, choosing to listen to Marcos instead.

Now, in the exact same spot, I was fighting to stake myself to the ground. To stop this spinning out of control. To tether myself in the fury of the whirlwind surrounding me. My voice was releasing as I was becoming, being shaped by the storm. I screamed, raising my voice to be free, over the winds of change. I screamed for mercy from the onslaught of the storm without end. It had been days since it all began with the phone call from the emergency room. I struggled to see the light I had known within me. I searched to remember the light that had consumed my being to overflowing, while I was in the hospital. The light had flowed freely, direct from the Source, without limit. I needed that light to guide me from this moment forward; it was the only way I could survive and make this life worth living. It was as if my eyes had been sealed shut – the light gone from my awareness completely – as I cried out for relief, for meaning and purpose.

I held on, steadfast in my commitment to myself in this moment, despite the chaos of emotions flooding my body. I was grasping for the calm I knew to be ever present in the heart of the storm. I was shattering to nothing, being broken, numbed by the waves bearing down on me. I couldn't see the light at the core of being, but I remembered. I knew the light could never leave me, could never be separated from who I am. I wouldn't give in, be consumed. I held fast, fixed my gaze upon my son and wouldn't let go.

The torrent could only last so long. With my lungs pounding, gasping for breath, I held on. All I wanted was to exhale, to breathe freely, to be freed from the pressure pressing inward. From this moment forward the healing would begin – I just had to survive this moment. I would remember who I was, remember my own strength. I would find peace within my heart again. I was stronger than I had ever known; I just had to remember who I was. I had to follow my heart back to my truth, back to the light within me.

No more would I be the passive child, the good girl, doing what everyone else expected. Marcos had always guided me. There was no questioning where we went, what we did. It was all under Marcos' control, his mood following his desires. He was never outwardly cruel, he never yelled, that was just how it was. If he said we weren't going, we weren't going. My attempts to persuade fell on deaf ears. He was the dominant; I was the submissive.

Everything was different now; everything had shifted. I was aware. I knew now that I had lost my voice, my power. I was finding my way back to choice, to myself. I was becoming aware that I had not consented to this transfer of power. That I had not intentionally stopped making choices. Each small concession I made led to another, and before I knew it, I had no personal boundaries remaining to protect me. I had no sense of self to declare or sustain. It was as if I had been under a spell, and the curse had been lifted. Magically, I was free overnight to create a new beginning. I hadn't sought this freedom. I didn't even know that I was a captive. I was a victim who had no idea I had been a victim. I was being given my freedom, and I resented it. I rejected and feared the ability to make my own choices. I wanted to reject this freedom, to go back to the safety and predictability of my captor.

I was forced now to find my own power within. I was standing up and saying no. No, I didn't care what the expectations were. No, I didn't need to please anyone to be loved or accepted. No, I wasn't going anywhere, doing anything or eating anything I didn't want to. I didn't care if people wanted to see Felipe. I didn't want anyone taking him out of my arms, crying and saying, "Poor mijito, you have no father." I would stand up for him, as I had not done for myself. He was not a poor, fatherless child. He had me – I was coming back. I would be present for him, as I hadn't been for myself.

People kept coming to the door, pressing for me to go to the reception. I was supposed to be present, to let others grieve, hug me and give their condolences. They wanted to comfort and be comforted, to give love that I was not able to receive. I was pushing them away, isolating myself out of preservation for what little of me remained. I had to survive to take care of my son. I couldn't give any more away. I had to stand up and I had to do it now.

I held on to survival mode, fully entrenched in the desire to live. I didn't trust anyone or anything. My mind played tricks on me. My inner voice turned the pain inward, punishing myself. I made myself believe nobody wanted me; they wanted Felipe. I didn't matter. I knew they were frustrated, worried, fearful they would lose him, that I would leave and return to New York with my family. I couldn't offer them any comfort. I didn't know myself what I was going to do. I couldn't offer them a comfort I didn't possess. I couldn't think; I couldn't plan and create a new future, not now. I couldn't accept this moment. How could I create a future based on a moment I couldn't allow to be real? I was in the process of transformation and rebirth, phasing in and out of becoming who I was meant to be.

Act 2

Chapter 7

Back in Albuquerque

It was all over, the funeral, the burial and the reception. I was back home, in Albuquerque, trying to sleep through the night, unable to eat as people kept arriving. They continued to bring food as they had done only two months before, to celebrate the birth of Felipe. Within two months I was celebrating life and celebrating death.

The celebration was exactly the same. People gathering, offering to help clean the house, delivering home-cooked meals, sharing stories from the heart. Life and death brought people together. A desire for connection – to pause for a moment, to remember, reflect and celebrate all that is precious. Life is precious; birth and death both remind us of this precious gift. We are renewed, pressed equally to live a life of value and purpose by the reality of life and death.

Some who came embraced death, flowing with it, accepting it as a part of God's plan. Others struggled with death and came needing to know why it had happened. Why would God allow it? I wanted to know how. How did it happen? I read the coroner's report, the autopsy and the police report, analyzing and scrutinizing every detail. I wanted to know the sequence of events, the timing and the conclusions established.

I needed to feel what Marcos had felt. I needed to understand how he was seen by the doctors, medical examiners and police. I wanted to see, through his eyes, those final moments. I wanted to see how strangers saw him, versus the way I saw the man that I knew. I wanted to see and experience every possible perspective of that day. I had to put it all together like a puzzle, pulling the missing pieces from each perspective to make a whole I could accept.

I had to feel and experience what Marcos had felt and experienced in his last moments. I needed to go through all of it, spare myself nothing of what Marcos had endured. I had to feel, through the words on those pages, what Marcos saw, what he heard and what he was aware or not aware of. I needed to experience the coroner's eyes examining his body, as though I were the one lying on that slab.

Marcos had made a right-hand turn at the red light at the end of our street. A young kid, newly licensed with his friend in the car, had forgotten something at his house. They turned around and were racing back across Zuni, a four-lane road with two lanes in each direction, to get back home. They sped through, attempting to cross all four lanes at once.

Marcos was alone in the last lane. The right turn on a red light from the street intersecting Zuni separated him from the rest of the traffic. Marcos was going less than twenty-five miles per hour when he struck the car, ripping his leg from his hip socket. His body was torn from the motorcycle and flung across the hood of the car. His body crashed to the pavement on the other side of the car. His head struck the edge of the curb of the intersecting street, with no helmet to shield his fall.

He had made peace with this long before the accident ever happened. He had declared he would rather be dead than crippled, if he ever had an accident on the motorcycle. This was in response to my request that he wear a helmet, now that we had a son. Though I protested that he needed to take responsibility, his decision didn't change. His choice was final. It always was, I knew that. I did all I could to stop this inevitable sequence of events, but it was not to be.

Paramedics

I heard the paramedics racing to the scene. It happened a block from our home. Moments later I was getting the phone call, knowing it was my number on Marcos' pager. There was no one else I paged but Marcos. There was no other person it could have been when the nurse called that day from the emergency room.

The paramedics had said that he was never conscious. It was explained to me later that the pain of the leg being ripped from the hip socket had probably caused him to black out. He had never felt anything. He was gone before his head ever hit the curb. I believe his spirit left his body at the moment of impact. He was gone long before I arrived at the emergency room. Only his body lingered to give us time to adapt to the change that had already happened.

A few years earlier I had been out riding my bicycle, in upstate New York. A German Shepherd had come across my path. I had encountered him many times before. I would kick my leg out and yell at him to leave me alone, so I could speed past his house. This time he got smart. He ran up ahead where I couldn't reach him with my foot. The last thing I remember was a truck coming towards me in the opposite lane, in oncoming traffic, and the dog racing toward me.

I remember the paramedics asking me my address and who to call. I remember saying words then slipping away again. I didn't feel anything. I had no awareness of what had happened or why anyone was asking me questions. I had a groggy sense of people around me, and movement in my peripheral vision –

that was it. I came to in the hospital, lying in a bed, with my mom at my side.

I had just received a brand-new helmet, days before my accident, as a gift from an ex-boyfriend who had received it for free at a bike event. It was Styrofoam only, with no outer shell. It was for survival, not style. It was a new concept in the biking community. I had never worn a helmet before that. It was the early '90s and that wasn't a part of my awareness.

I learned later that a woman had been sitting on her front porch that summer evening and had seen it all. She said that I never let go of the bike. I flipped, bike and all, and landed on my head. She thought I was dead; that there was no way I could have survived. When she went to me, I was still holding the handlebars of the bike. She called the volunteer fire department to come and get me. I was out in the countryside, and they were the closest emergency response team available. I never remembered the details of the accident; I felt no pain at the time of impact. I never felt a thing until I woke up in the ER. That was all I knew for certain.

I drew comfort from this experience, confirming my belief that Marcos had never felt a thing. He never knew what happened. He saw a car and was gone. The paramedics let me know he was never conscious. I had not missed any last words. It was consciousness that brought awareness. Without awareness there was no experience to be drawn by the mind. Without consciousness there could be no pain, no trauma, no emotions of fear and terror to take hold. There could be no memory of the experience if the mind was not conscious.

Marcos Knew

Marcos knew he was going to die. I was convinced of this fact. The night before the accident I was lying on the couch, looking at Felipe lying next to me. I could hear Marcos behind us in his recliner, crying. I looked back and said, "Pea, why are you crying, what's wrong?" He said, "I just love you guys so much." He was sobbing. He pulled off his glasses and wiped away the tears. I laughed at him, teasing him, saying how much we loved him too. He was so sweet and sentimental, especially since Felipe had been born.

He loved his son so much that he had an image of him tattooed on his stomach. Felipe lay in a bassinet, and two angels, one on either side, held swords drawn in protection. The image took up the space of his entire stomach, up to his ribs. Here he was, watching us, crying, saying how much he loved us. I drew confidence from this later, as I reflected on the days preceding the accident. He knew he was going to die. This was Marcos saying goodbye.

The morning of the accident, I begged Marcos, holding Felipe in my arms, not to go to work that day.

I said "Don't go today, stay with us. Don't go to work." He was leaving early, and he was in a rush to get going. Something about the hurry to get out the door triggered my need for him to stay. Some message was being sent from deep within me, telling me to grasp hold of this moment, to stop the spinning that was beginning to take hold.

Why was he in such a rush if he was early? Why was I begging him to stay home? I had never before asked him to stay home and not to go to work. Not once had I requested he not go when he was about to leave. That day, though, I stood up and asked him not to leave. I begged him to stay home. He raced out the door anyway, his motorcycle warming up in front of the house. He always made his own choices; he wasn't going to stop now.

As Marcos was about to go to work, despite my protests, he stopped and came back into the house. He had forgotten to tell me something, "I'm not going to be home tonight," he stated as fact. I asked, "What are you talking about?" He replied, "I mean, I'm going to get a tattoo, and I won't be home until around 10:30. I forgot to mention it to you the other day." As always, I accepted what he said without question. Not only was he not staying, as I had begged, he wouldn't be home tonight, or at least not until 10:30.

In response to my disappointment, as if I had expressed doubt as to the truth of his words, he pulled a postcard from his pocket. The card had a picture of an Aztec warrior holding his love in his arms, while leaning her back as if to kiss her exposed neck. When I hesitated – looking at the image, puzzled, as I had never seen it before – he expressed that the image was supposed to represent the two of us. I didn't understand what he meant, as he was a mix of Aztec, Spanish and Mexican, a native of New Mexico – and I was white, Anglo, with a mix of European blood. How could this image represent us? It was an Aztec couple. Again, I didn't question his motives, and I only accepted what I was told. Marcos turned and left for the last time, saying nothing more.

    Everything was moving exactly as planned. All the pieces were set in place. Marcos had to leave at exactly that moment, to catch the red light, to turn before all the traffic. To meet the car speeding back, crossing the lanes it had just cleared. They were going to make it before that one motorcycle came too close. They had to hurry or they would miss their chance. All the cars would be coming and they would be stuck waiting for traffic, instead of racing back home for the CD they had left behind.

    I didn't know until much later that this kid knew Marcos. Marcos had driven a school bus for mission trips to Mexico, and the kid driving the car had been one of those kids he had taken to Mexico. Marcos had known him. On this fateful day, he and Marcos were racing to meet each other on that exact piece of pavement. I had been begging Marcos not to go, the kid forgetting his CD. The timing was perfect. It was meant to be. It was beyond coincidence.

All of it played out together for this one perfect moment. I heard the sirens as I was putting Felipe down to sleep. It was just down the road and around the corner. I paused for a moment, hearing the sirens, and continued on with what I was doing. I heard the paramedics as they were rushing to the scene, and only gave it a moment's notice, a glance in time. We were all connected in that one singular moment, without knowing it.

Marcos had premonitions, days before the accident. He and I were sitting on the floor by Felipe as he rocked back and forth in his swing. Marcos told me he wished he could see my father meet Felipe for the first time. I was confused. I looked at him and said, "You will." He said, "No. I won't be home when your dad arrives." I said, "What do you mean?" He replied, "I will be at work." It seemed like nothing at the time – a mere moment of confusion quickly sorted and put to rest.

Luna had a premonition the morning of the accident. She went out the door to go to work, and there were birds everywhere. A large flock of black birds had landed in her driveway. She got into the car and drove down the road. There were hundreds of birds all over the road. She had never seen anything like it before. She thought of Marcos at that moment, and thought she had better call to check on him and tell him about the birds. But she went on to work, and didn't make the call.

Marcos' boss at the salon had talked to him about getting a life-insurance policy, and had helped him complete the application, weeks before the accident. His boss knew he had a family, and should have a plan in place, in case anything ever happened to him. The policy went into effect on April 1, 1996. I could see how the insurance company would question his death at age thirty-two, a day after purchasing a life insurance policy for $100,000. His birthday was July 1, 1963; our anniversary was May 21, 1995; Felipe had been born in January, 1996 and Marcos was declared dead at 10:30 pm on April 2, 1996. The timing was impeccable; pure precision with no wasted moments.

I came to Albuquerque based on a dream – a dream where I was living in an adobe home with a baby. Here I was, a single mom alone with a son, living in a traditional adobe-style home. It was all playing out along a preordained path. Little signs were strewn along the way; I paid no notice. All these little signs were to become a blessing to me. They were the confirmation that everything was perfect, even if it didn't go as I had planned. It had been foretold and was predetermined. Everything would be all right; life was unfolding as planned. This is what gave me solace. Marcos knew, I knew and Luna knew. The universe had prepared me through it all without my noticing.

I had even had a premonition myself a few days earlier, as I was washing the dishes. One of those quick, flashing thoughts of Marcos dying, with the insurance money in place as planned. I quickly banished the thought, thinking that it was all this talk of life insurance, contingencies to pay off the SUV loan and requests for Marcos to wear a helmet that were making me paranoid that something was going to happen.

These are all the talks you have when you become a new parent. In hindsight, it felt as if we had created it. We talked about it, we planned for it and it happened right on cue. Marcos had even told me he was stashing away our marriage license and other important documents under a dresser drawer, so I would know where they were if I needed them. I still have no idea why he would hide those documents to make them safe. Why would anyone want to steal them?

I completely forgot where he told me they were after he passed. My mom, sister and I tore the house apart, trying to find them, after the funeral. I was in a complete panic, crying that I couldn't even prove we were married. It hadn't even been a year. I struggled to come to terms with the understanding that perfect isn't always what I think it should be. Life doesn't always go as planned. My mom pulled the drawer out of the dresser in her search and found the papers.

Chapter 8

Good Days

In the days that followed, everyone returned to their routines and I was left alone with Felipe. I was left to go about living once more. I would meet strangers who were kind, and I would pour out my heart, connecting from deep within my soul. Confirming, "Everything is perfect, beautiful, in accord with the Divine plan." There were moments when I felt surrounded in peace, love, compassion and support. I felt embraced, as I had been that day in the hospital, in a bubble of Divine protection and blessing. I was waiting for the miracle to be revealed to me still. I knew a gift had to be hidden within this experience. I just had to find it.

On my good days I knew I was never truly alone, never beyond repair, never apart from love. I knew the light within me was greater than any darkness I could ever know. I connected with others, openly sharing stories of love and compassion. This made everything I had experienced worth it. I was alive, protected, loved. When my angels were with me keeping me safe, that was a good day.

Shortly after the accident, I received a call from an insurance agent saying that Marcos was on drugs at the time of his death. They had decided they wouldn't pay out the life insurance. I became infuriated, and told the insurance agent that Marcos had been pumped full of morphine at the hospital to make certain he would feel no pain when the machines were shut off. I told him to confirm with the hospital that this was true. I stood firm. I couldn't believe the accusation, and how callously he declared his belief as fact. This man chose to call me and make this devastating statement of denial, rather than call the hospital for an explanation to confirm or deny his suspicion.

The insurance company researched their accusation and conceded that Marcos had not been on drugs at the time of the accident. He never did drugs, smoked or touched alcohol. It was all part of his promise to God, to live a new life in payment for a second chance after escaping death, when he returned from the army addicted to drugs, with hepatitis B and his liver shutting down.

I have found that there are beautiful, compassionate souls, full of love, who reach out in kindness when they are needed most. And there are those, caught up in their jobs and their titles, who are not trusting, not empathizing, who are cruel and unkind without reason. They do not touch death and suffering. They look the other way. They do not feel it, accept it or embrace it. They judge, hurl insults and race the other way as fast as possible, without regard for the damage and devastation they leave in their wake.

Bad Days

On my bad days I experienced the dark thoughts of a soul untethered. I would cry out in pain, isolation and loneliness. I wanted desperately to return to the known, the comfortable, the secure, the way life used to be. I became frightened of the future. I would cry out to God to hold me safe in his arms. Broken on the floor, I sobbed, until there were no more tears to cry.

When the tears stopped, peace returned. There was nothing left. I had emptied my heart upon the floor – the tears, the pain, the sorrow, the torment. When it had passed I would get up, keep moving forward, make tea, do the chores. I lived the mundane, day-to-day life again. I continued, I survived. That part of my soul that broke and lingered still in that hospital room was released, so that I could survive, continue forward, carry on, and be here on this Earth in this experience. A part of me broke in half, so that the whole could survive.

On my bad days, I made myself believe that Luna wanted to take Felipe from me and raise him as her own. That she resented me, believing I had allowed them to pull the plug on the machines. That she didn't want me around. That it was my fault that Marcos was gone. I was a reminder that all the plans they had made would never be fulfilled. All she had done, however, was offer to help raise Felipe, so that I could move on in my life and have a fresh start. But I pushed her away, made her the villain in my mind. I thought this is what I had to do to be strong. I had to be alone, not ask for help, not rely on anyone. I had to make my own decisions, and stop letting everyone else tell me what was best for me and my child.

Luna couldn't understand. I was a different person – I had shifted, transformed. I was born again. I was given a second chance at life. I had awoken from the illusion, the false reality I had created, that I was weak and powerless, and needed protecting; that I couldn't take care of myself and that I didn't have dreams of my own. I had purpose; I had a child to raise. I was committed to finding my direction.

The night Marcos passed, when I couldn't find my way home, something inside me snapped. My darkest hour was my hour of transformation and rebirth. I realized I was lost. I accepted it. I could see it clearly. I acknowledged my part in the choices I made. I decided quietly within my heart that I needed to stand up, take responsibility for my life. I was not a victim. I had made the choice to not speak up for myself. I had not set healthy boundaries to be respected. No one in New Mexico had seen me be strong, say no, set boundaries or stand up for myself. I was a different person now. I had changed overnight. As Marcos was dying, I was given life.

I loved him with all my heart; he never intentionally tried to harm me. We were acting in ignorance, fear and low self-esteem, and without confidence in who we were meant to be. This was what I had allowed to happen in my life. He wanted to create a life with me, a future. He was afraid of losing me, and I didn't set boundaries. I couldn't blame him for my weakness, my lack of self-esteem. He did his part and I did mine. He didn't see me as weak. He wanted me as his partner, and he wanted to be loved by me. He was afraid of losing me. He wanted me to be happy, to share his dreams for the future. He wanted me to be a great artist. He was proud of me and all that I created. I tried to blame his strength, his confidence and bravado, for my weakness. My power was taken from me piece by piece, and I resented him for taking it so willingly.

Harley Repaired

My newfound strength and resolve continued to be tested. Marcos' motorcycle had been impounded at the time of the accident. I had not thought about it since the accident. I received a call that Marcos' cousin was having the motorcycle taken to his house. He intended to fix it up for himself, without asking me. I couldn't believe he was trying to do this without my consent.

His cousin was at the impound, actively trying to put the bike on a trailer to take home, when I arrived. I was adamant that he didn't have the authority to do so. It was time for me to take responsibility for my actions and stop blaming those around me for what I was experiencing. I had to be strong – there was no concession for anything *but* strength. I was Marcos' wife. I was the one to decide where the bike went. The bike was my personal property. I instructed the owner of the impound to have the bike sent to Chick's Harley-Davidson to be repaired by the insurance company and made ready to sell. The owner of the impound conceded that I alone had authority to make the decision, and he had the bike delivered for repairs as I had instructed.

The loan for our SUV had been paid in full at the time of Marcos' death. The bank had offered Marcos an insurance rider on the policy to pay off the SUV loan in case of his death. I remembered saying to Marcos, what would I do if something happened to him? There was no way, on my UNM work-study income, that I could pay the SUV loan and the motorcycle loan. Marcos agreed, and added the coverage on the SUV.

Marcos had intended to go back and add the rider to the motorcycle. Money was tight after the wedding and the birth of our son, and he wasn't able to cover the premium on the additional insurance rider for the motorcycle. When Marcos began having trouble making payments, the motorcycle was advertised in the local car rags for sale and proof given to the bank that he was attempting to sell the bike. So many attempts had been made to avert the accident – but that wasn't meant to be.

I was lost, struggling to find my power, vulnerable. Marcos had always handled these matters. He never shared with me the condition of our finances. I was now staying at home, and no longer had an income at all. I was dependent on Marcos to pay the bills and provide a home for us. It was a fight to do even the most basic errands. Marcos drove, everywhere; I had no idea where I needed to go to get things done. I had no memory of the streets, no geography, no map in my mind.

Weeks after I had the motorcycle delivered for repair, I drove for hours trying to find the Harley store, to check on the repairs to the bike. I drove in circles trying to find my way. With Felipe crying, I returned home; then I rested, cried, ate and tried again. I failed again and returned home, and with frustration overwhelming me I cried out to God, feeling pity for myself and my self-inflicted isolation. I broke upon the floor once more, crying out in my struggle to become strong, independent and self-reliant. I cried until there were no more tears, no victim remaining.

I was broken, but something inside me couldn't surrender. Deep within my being, I was a survivor. Some part of me continued to fight, wouldn't give up. There was no one to call. This was my responsibility. I tried again. After hours of driving, I found my way across town. It was my choice to give up or continue moving forward. I accepted where I was. I forgave my weakness, rested and continued to fight. I arrived at the store exhausted, frustrated and emotionally drained.

I entered the store carrying Felipe in my arms. I asked for help to be directed to the back where Marcos' bike was being repaired. The people who worked in the store were hesitant, afraid of what to say to me. They watched as I entered; whispers followed. I was the wife of the biker who had died. I was holding our infant son in my arms. I was the one having the bike repaired, I was the face no one wanted to see. I was the symbol of the reality of consequences for choices made.

They knew I had to sell the bike to pay off the loan; they were doing their best to help make that happen. I smiled, sympathetic to their struggle, and expressed my appreciation for all that they were doing and how great the bike looked. I pretended that nothing had happened. I said nothing of my pain. I said nothing of the consequences of not wearing a helmet in an attempt at looking cool.

The bike sold quickly. It was less than a year old, and the repairs made it look brand new. I paid the loan in full with proceeds I received from the sale of the motorcycle. The outstanding loan balance was $16,000 dollars. It sold for $16,583, enough to cover the debt. Had I not been adamant, stood up for myself, I would have been stuck with that debt to pay.

I was a single mom, living thousands of miles away from my home and family, and struggling to finish college and get my degree. My emotions vacillated between being elated, happy and free while fully coming back into my own power, to lying broken on the floor in despair. crying out to Marcos and to God for answers.

No Money

I had no money. I thought I had access to the bank accounts. Marcos had told them to add me to the account. I thought I had signed the paper to be added, but they had no record at the bank of that ever happening. I had been writing checks and signing them, never knowing that I wasn't on the account. The bank explained that they never looked at the checks, as no complaints had been filed about unauthorized checks. The accounts were closed; Marcos had died. I needed a death certificate to release the funds. That would take time and bureaucracy to get by mail. I had a credit card in my name from before I met Marcos; this was all I had for money. This was twenty years ago and grocery stores didn't take credit cards.

I was forced to trust each moment as it arrived. My fear of storms had faded; acceptance made it easier to become the observer of my experience. What I needed was provided, when I needed it. There was nothing else for me to do but surrender to the flow of life. I was adrift and figuring out each new step as it was presented to me. I had to become patient, trust the timing and allow others to help.

Marcos was a hairdresser, so he would get tips on top of his wages. The salon set up a tip jar in honor of Marcos after the funeral, and sent the money to me. I received a couple hundred dollars to buy food. I never told anyone my situation. They had no idea how dependent I was on their gifts of charity. I was doing the best I could with a new baby and no income. I needed diapers and all the expenses that come with an infant. I went to the Women Infant and Children (WIC) office and applied for assistance.

The woman sitting across from me said that my husband made too much money; our tax return showed too much income. I said, "He's dead. I have no paychecks from him. I quit my work-study job at the college toward the end of my pregnancy, so I had no income either." She stared at me for a moment before she relented and approved my application. I would receive benefits until I could get my life-insurance payment and Social Security payments in place.

I learned, with WIC, to buy the cheapest versions of the allowed foods. The cheapest canned grape juice, the cheapest block of cheese and generic tuna. I learned what I could and could not buy by trial and error at the checkout line. The foods that the government gives you to choose from were not healthy at all. I followed the guidelines and bought what I could. I would carry Felipe in my arm and push the cart with my other hand, balancing it all, as I reached for items to place in my cart.

My professors at school let me slide and finish the rest of the semester with the paintings I had already submitted for review. I was grateful. I wouldn't lose all the work I had done over the last semester and have to repeat my classes. I was getting stronger, becoming more independent and finding my way back to my power. I was receiving support and encouragement in the most unexpected places.

I had not realized how weak I had become. I had let Marcos decide everything. It was his house, his things, his friends, his life. I had merged into his life, given up my voice and lived through him. Even the simplest decisions seemed monumental without him. I was struggling for the sake of my son to find my way to create a new life for the both of us.

The insurance money was finally sorted out, and it arrived as a check in the mail a few months after Marcos' death. I was able to get the Social Security benefits in place once I received the death certificates and could show them as proof of death. Everything needed a certificate: birth, marriage, death. I had them all now to show to everyone who needed them. It was as if my life had to be fully documented before I had any hope of moving forward. I was free now. I was gaining strength, asking questions, finding my way and creating balance in my life. I was a survivor. I had the strength within me make to it through to the other side.

Chapter 9

The New Apartment

While I waited for all the bureaucracy to be sorted out, I had begun going through the house, gathering loads of belongings for local charities. I would load up my front porch again and again with possessions I no longer needed, and have Goodwill and others come to take it all away. Marcos was a pack rat. He had pots, pans, books and plain old junk that was not needed. I went through it all. Everything special, or an important part of Marcos' life – his travels as a missionary, any memories – I kept. The rest I gave away. I did weeks of laborious work while Felipe took his naps.

I was alone, and this kept me busy and distracted while giving me a sense of accomplishment. After my bouts of crying, there was nothing left to do but reflect and reclaim this space as my own. I didn't recognize this as home without Marcos. There was virtually nothing of mine in the place.

I came to New Mexico with nothing more than a trunk full of belongings, mostly clothes and some items I held precious from hiking and exploring in nature. I was surrounded by black lacquer and brass furniture, glass table tops; nothing natural. No wood, stones, or natural fabrics. All of it was flashy sateen and velvet; purple, black, burgundy and emerald green.

That was not my taste; Marcos had picked it all out before and after we were married. I loved him as he was; he had his own style, flair and personality. My choices were completely different. It was time to express my individuality. It was time to let go of that which did not express who I was becoming, and who I already was at my core.

I reduced everything to the bare minimum, and put the rest in storage. I didn't get rid of anything that would mean something to his mom, his family or Felipe when he was old enough. I saved his clothes, everything he was actively using at the time of his death. I collected the remnants of his life and moved them to storage. I separated myself from the identity I had assumed, and began creating an awareness of my own preferences and choices.

I moved into a small apartment with the basics: bed, dresser, entertainment center, kitchen table, Felipe's crib, dressing table and a trunk for toys. I bought a new couch and put the old one in storage. I left lots of space on the floor for Felipe and me to play. Marcos' family kept in touch, but they left me alone to figure out my new life. They knew I was going to make my own decisions. I knew they were there if Felipe or I were ever in need. The storm was long past; my need for hope to sustain me had been released. I was facing reality as it was, accepting it all. I was creating, expressing, feeling the sun upon my skin and enjoying life again.

All my baby weight was gone. I was back to 115 pounds. The loss of the initial twenty pounds triggered the release of the remaining weight. I had reduced my portions, and my appetite was gone. I had to buy less to make ends meet. Once I had my funds sorted out, I was making healthier choices, in response to the awful foods permitted on WIC. The extreme of the inferior and unhealthy foods I experienced in the months immediately following Marcos' death pushed me back to the healthy choices and lifestyle I had known as a child.

I was beginning to find my freedom, to live again – to follow my own path, dreams and desires. I was happy and alive, and Felipe was with me always. We played, we laughed, he was beautiful. I continued to go deep within my pain and bounce back anew, knowing a little bit more about myself, my strength and my ability for compassion. My self-esteem and confidence were growing moment by moment, as I accepted my mistakes, forgave myself and took responsibility for my future.

I realized that life was a gift, each moment precious. There were no mistakes, only lessons to be learned along the way. My perception of the accident changed with time. It was horrible, traumatic and profound. With acceptance I embraced it as a vital turning point in my life. I began to see it as a blessing that tore me apart, showed me I was lost and helped me find my way by following my internal compass, my light within. Compassion and forgiveness for myself and others began to bloom within my heart. I was finding my purpose, my passion once more.

My connection to the Earth and the hearts of others was being restored. It was a soul-breaking experience that left me connected, realigned, in tune with my own direction. I began creating a life of value and purpose. I reached out – and love reached back. I will always be thankful. I thought I was gone. The whole time I was waiting deep within for my own return.

Fight with Luna

Time was passing in bouts of good days and bad. As the months passed, the good days were far outweighing the bad. I began engaging in my surroundings, enjoying my last classes at the university and connecting with new and old friends.

Luna would come to Albuquerque on the bus and stay for periods of time. Sometimes weeks, sometimes only a few days over the weekend – whatever she could manage and still continue to work full time as a schoolteacher. We would spend hours sitting at the kitchen table getting to know one another, sharing stories of our childhoods. We were so much alike in so many ways.

Luna had come and was staying the weekend at my new apartment. It had been less than a year since Marcos' death. I had started spending time with a cousin of Marcos' who was kind to me. We had always gotten along well when we would see each other at family events. Ryan lived in Albuquerque and wasn't much older than me. He had completed his degree at the University only a few months before, and he had gotten a great job right out of school. He would have Felipe and me over for dinner and take me out to his work events. It was nice to have a friend – and with time, it developed into something more than just friendship. Luna realized that her sister's son was spending time with me, and she was devastated.

We had the biggest fight I have ever experienced. She was enraged, indignant. I was supposed to be alone for a year, if not more. How could I do this to her and Marcos? I never loved him, she said. I was callous and insensitive. All of her feelings from that first moment in the hospital room, when she first laid eyes on Marcos, came flooding back.

All of the venom was pouring out from her pain and suffering at the loss of her son and best friend. She had hidden it, held it back, but in this moment the full torrent was being unleashed. She was enraged; the full, boiling emotions had finally found a place to be released. She wanted to leave, go back to Taos. She demanded I take her to the bus depot immediately. I said no, that she was not leaving. Marcos would not want that. I stood up in the storm of her fury. I defied her as no one else dared to. I stood in her path and would not give in. I had found the strength within me to survive in the face of the storm, in the chaos of raging emotions, and I called upon that strength in this moment.

In the midst of it all a voice, still and calm, emerged inside me. I began to pray within my heart for love, to have compassion for her suffering, and to allow healing to take place. I asked in my heart that she feel my love. The venom continued pouring out from her, yet in my own heart I returned the poison with love. I held on and would not let go. I knew from my own crying out on the floor in weakness that it could last only so long. She relented; she only had so much venom, so much rage, that she could release at one time. The storm had poured all it had to offer; it had run its course. Calm and peace had returned once more. She accepted me as I was, and I embraced her as she was. I told her I loved her, and I held her close. She had exhausted her fight to resist, to not accept what had happened. She surrendered, and began her path toward healing, one step at a time.

I had passed the greatest test – the test of compassion for a fellow human being in suffering – and survived. I held my peace and did not attack. I felt compassion for her suffering, instead of feeling defensive of my sense of freedom, choices and decisions. I connected with my heart and held a place of stillness in the storm. The venom of pure hate directed straight at me could not destroy the unconditional love and compassion welling, bubbling up from within. My strength was returning. I was remembering who I am in the midst of the storm. I forgave myself for hurting her so deeply. I forgave her the pain she had no other way to release. I allowed the moment to be perfect the way it was.

I began living on purpose, following my heart's desire. I had no worries about finances, deadlines; nothing caused me stress. I went to class during the day, taking two or three classes a semester. I took an independent-study course, so that I could work from home. I brought my artwork for reviews, with Felipe in tow – taking trips to and from the car repeatedly until I had carried it all up the stairs to the professor's office, and doing the same afterwards to get it all back home again.

Things were good. I had found a woman who cared for children in her home to help me with Felipe when I couldn't bring him with me. I was expanding, living free with Felipe. I had a friend in my life who was supportive, not controlling. I had surrendered to my newfound independence and freedom. I was making plans for the future and creating a life for myself.

All the experiences I had endured were crucial to my understanding and recognizing my pattern in life.

They were critical to my finding the direction of the path I was on. My experiences forced me to find my intention to live life on purpose, to create value and meaning. I loved Marcos, and I had surrendered completely, becoming him and losing myself. In response to his death I sought my own freedom and independence. To obtain it, I turned those who wanted to help me into enemies, so that I could stand on my own two feet.

The experiences I faced forced me to find a way to survive – but survival wasn't enough; breathing wasn't enough reason to live and endure the struggle. I turned to love to find my way; to give life meaning, value and purpose. Love did not disappoint me. Love never left my side in my darkest hours. Love did not feed me expectations that could not be accepted. Love found a way to help me heal, to find my light, to extend compassion to myself and others. Love helped me to forgive it all, including myself.

Without the storm, my transformation – my life pattern – would never have been revealed. The devastation reignited my internal compass; it caused me to seek the light within my heart. The silence, the stillness after the storm created a space for me to listen. I heard, I stood up, I took back my power and began life anew. I said no. I created boundaries to be respected. I demanded a space to *be* and began expanding outward. My channel had begun to open, allowing the energy of love, of life, to flow through me.

Act 3

Chapter 10
I'm Pregnant

I looked myself squarely in the face and said, "My God, I'm pregnant." I don't know how I knew, but I did. Standing in the hotel bathroom of the Ramada Inn (which a friend kept erroneously calling the Ramona Inn), I used the bathroom, cleaned up, climbed back into bed next to Peter and waited for the storm to unleash its fury in the coming weeks. I said not a word of what I knew was coming.

I had decided to go on a trip to New York City – a friend of Peter's was getting married. It was a beautiful wedding, held at a private country estate. I met a stylist couple at the wedding who had named their dog after the blue lake, held sacred to the Taos Pueblo. The wedding concluded with a gorgeous display of fireworks. I tried to dance with Peter at the end of the evening, but he had been drinking to the point of being drunk and wanted to goof off. I walked away before he could embarrass me.

It was the morning after the wedding when I stood before the mirror in the hotel room, my life shifting before my eyes. I had not let my new pattern of independence solidify into my being before I began a new relationship, after Marcos' death. I had not found my pattern. I hadn't recognized the root of my lack of self-esteem and confidence. I hadn't taken the time to be alone, to listen to my heart and find what my dreams and goals were. I hadn't taken the time to gain awareness and cement it firmly into my being. I rushed in, not wanting to be alone – not wanting to create my own joy or make my own decisions. I was still not ready to create a life of value of my own choosing.

That morning, Peter had sex with me. We were sharing a room with his friends, who had asked in advance that he respect their boundaries and not have sex in the room. I'm convinced he was still drunk from the night before when he rolled over to me. I should have stopped him, stood up, left the bed. I didn't want to create a scene. It was over before it began. I got up to use the bathroom – and that was when I knew, without hesitation, without question, that I was pregnant. The storm was upon me.

A month later, my period did not arrive on schedule – just as I'd anticipated. I bought a pregnancy test, drove to the mountains, peed in the woods on the small white stick and confirmed what I already knew. I was pregnant. On the drive back into town, all I could say to myself was, "My God, I'm going to have to buy another car seat." That was the moment of clarity for me, another car seat. Reality hit home in that one impending purchase. There would be two dependents upon me. Acceptance was with me, holding my hand, as I drove back to Luna's house.

I pulled the car into the drive; I had to tell Luna. The thoughts racing in my mind were, "I'm pregnant. I'm living at your house with my son. I'm not married and the father lives in Dallas." I stood in the doorway to the bathroom, as she was getting ready to leave for the day, and gave her the news direct and to the point, "I'm pregnant." That was it, no building up, no hinting at what it might be, just the bombshell.

To Luna's credit, she giggled and was immediately supportive. She was going to have another grandchild was her immediate response. In that moment I gained so much respect for Luna; her values and core beliefs, her love of family, were the cornerstone of her life. I became even closer to her and trusted her even more than I had before, having moved in with her only two months earlier. I then went to another room, called Peter and told him I was pregnant. He said he would take responsibility, that he was willing to marry me. He would return to New Mexico and we would create a life. That was it, problem solved.

I was pregnant, all because Peter had called one summer evening and asked me to go on a trip to New York City for a friend's wedding. It was my choice. I had chosen to maintain the friendship, despite how he treated me. My perfect world filled with self-esteem and confidence was threatened by a storm I never saw coming. I believe the reason I knew I was pregnant, the moment I looked in the mirror, was because I hadn't heeded the warnings, the signals, my internal messages to stay away. This guy was no good for me. I was not true to myself. I didn't listen to my heart. I didn't maintain my power. I gave it all away, one piece at a time, yet again.

    I had not encountered a storm like this before. It was deceptive; it threatened hail stones the size of golf balls; the skies were dark and threatening – but it barely raised a wind of conflict. I was tricked, lulled into believing that it had passed, that it was false. The fury was silently growing without concern or regard on my part. There were warning signs all along, marking the journey from the beginning, signaling the storm to come. I paid no heed, did nothing to protect or prepare myself for the rage of this relentless storm. My guard was down; I thought it had passed. I had faced it head on and found it false.

Chapter 11

I Met Peter

I met Peter in one of my last classes at the University, my final semester. He was full of energy; always running, laughing and playing with his dog. He was an artist who shared my love of freedom and the possibility of adventure. My friendship with Marcos' cousin had ended; he wanted what I could not give, asking me to marry him and create a family. I moved forward in trust, hoping to find the freedom and adventure I desired.

Peter and I developed a friendship that never threatened my security or status quo. I was not his focus. I was more of a friend than a serious relationship. He would look at me and ask, "Why are you doing this traditional stuff? Be free, go to the mountains, find adventures." He was a dreamer, free from responsibility. My entire world turned upside down when I met him. He was the opposite of anything I had known.

We went on road trips, discovered new restaurants, traveled. I accepted that I paid all the expenses; gas, eating out, supplies – everything. He was happy, so I was happy. We took trips on the spur of the moment. Explored unknown mountain roads and travelled to distant cities and towns. I thought we were a couple, but we were not. He never calmed down, got serious or talked from the heart, except about how much he loved his ex-girlfriend Anastasia. Almost the same name as mine, one letter separated her from me. I supported and encouraged him through his grief that she had left him for another. I had been left and heartbroken too.

Graduated College

I graduated college, all my classes complete. Instead of attending the graduation, with no friends or family to be present, I went camping in Utah with Peter. No one had created any celebration or fanfare for my hard-fought graduation, so I skipped it. I went to Taos and bought myself a pair of feather earrings; hand carved out of bone and painted with the finest detailing. One of Marcos' aunts sold them to me, on the Taos Plaza, for a discounted price of $21. They are the symbol of my strength to endure, and complete my degree, against the odds. My sister Katelyn sent me a beautiful Blue Morpho butterfly, dried and placed in a glass frame. My graduation had been commemorated in my own way.

Luna loved to have time with Felipe, and she was excited that she could spend time with him for a week, while I went camping. I bought all the necessary provisions. I had not been camping since Marcos and I went fishing in the Taos mountains for a weekend. I never stopped to take notice that I was paying for everything. We were driving my car. I paid for all the gas and food. I was excited, having fun, exploring, on an adventure. We were unlimited, so long as I had the funds to pay. We extended the vacation from one week to two. I was no longer placing Felipe as my top priority, and Luna was spending more time with him. This would never have happened a year ago. It was good for their relationship, and for her healing. I didn't pause to consider what was happening. I never stepped back and became the observer, the witness of my own experience. I never looked within, never watched for the pattern emerging, the single lesson that I had come to experience in a myriad of ways.

I loved my new, expanded freedom that I experienced with Peter. He was always open and ready for adventure. There was always something new to do, some distant far-off place that would delight. I went on spontaneous trips, flying to New York City with Peter to visit his friends, going camping in the mountains and taking day trips all over New Mexico.

Shortly after I graduated college, I flew back to visit my family back in upstate New York with Felipe. It was good to go back to my mother's home and feel the growth I had experienced. My hair was growing out, and I had let the natural color return. I was beginning to feel like my old self again, only stronger, more confident than before.

When I left, and returned to New Mexico after my trip, I had decided that New York no longer offered what I was seeking. I was no longer interested in returning permanently to New York, now that I was finished with college. New Mexico was no longer a foreign land to me – it had become my home. It was now a place of adventure and possibility with Peter.

Chapter 12

Signs

The storm hovered high in the clouds above. It gave no cracking, thundering sounds of notice. There were no flashing lights of warning. I raced forward, believing I was beginning a new relationship. I was moving forward with my life without taking the time to plan, think ahead and create a blueprint for the future. I kept on going about my days, never pausing to look within.

In the beginning, when I was finishing college and had moved into my new apartment, I needed a new bed. I didn't want the black Laquerre bed I had when Marcos and I were married. I had just met Peter at the university, in one of my art classes. Peter needed money for a trip to Dallas. I spoke with him about making a bed for me and he agreed that he could do it. I gave him the money to build a new bed, $800. I wanted a bed made of wood with some of my artwork embedded in the headboard. Peter said he could do it, took the money, and went to Dallas to see his family and party with his friends. I thought nothing of it; the timing was never right after that to build the bed. He didn't have the tools or materials on hand. My bed never came. He took the money needed to build the bed, spent it on his trip, and never kept his promise.

Peter never gave me any reason to believe in him, or to trust him with my heart or my well-being. He was not a man of his word. Yet, he was not to blame. He fully disclosed who he was a thousand times. He took no responsibility for himself, or anyone else. He took my money without regret, letting me pay for everything, a single mom five years younger than him. I chose not to listen. I refused to heed the warnings he gave. This was my creation, what I allowed in my life, how I allowed myself to be treated. I take responsibility, accept what was and forgive my need for love outside of myself. I forgive my lack of self-worth. I forgive my lack of confidence.

I gave away my self-esteem, my value and worth, when I didn't say no to having sex with him the morning after the wedding. Despite the protests of his friends sharing the room, I said nothing. I pretended that confidence had nothing to do with it. I allowed him to disrespect me, and created the perfect environment for my victimization. I was being treated as I believed I deserved. Somehow I was not worthy of love, though I sought it desperately.

The First Warning

The warnings given were not subtle. The storm never attempted to hide its true potential. I became complacent. I was not decisive, not committed to my direction or myself. I was not listening to my heart, my inner voice of wisdom. As I reflect back, the warnings were all so clear, marking my flesh with their constant pressure.

After I finished college, Felipe and I moved to Edwards, Colorado with Peter, following one of our spontaneous trips. Peter led me to believe that everything would be better if we moved away from Marcos' family and all the baggage of my experiences in New Mexico. I followed Peter's dream to live in the small ski-resort town, leaving Albuquerque, New Mexico behind. I thought we would continue what we had started in New Mexico when I graduated from college. I wasn't listening, wasn't allowing myself to see the darkness in front of me.

I paid for everything the entire time we lived in Colorado. Peter did not earn a single cent. He did not contribute in any way to the expenses we created. I was a stay-at-home mom, a single parent, and I had to pay for everything. The entire time we lived together, Peter was distant, on the computer and playing games all day. I even paid for a spontaneous trip to San Francisco, to visit a friend of Peter's. My car broke down; everything that could go wrong did. I was draining money like a faucet wide open, not taking any heed of the signs I was experiencing. I took no action to protect myself.

We lasted in Colorado from November to March. By the end of March, Peter had decided he was going to move, leave Colorado without me, and return to Dallas where his family lived. He felt guilty not having any money and he wasn't having fun anymore. I said I would come with him; there was nothing for me in Colorado. I had no friends, no connections. Peter showed no signs that he wanted me to come with him when he moved to Dallas. I followed anyway. He led me to believe we would get a place together when I paid for the U-Haul and packed all of our belongings for the move.

My first solid warning slapped me in the face, as I was sitting at the kitchen table across from Peter's mother in her home in Dallas, Texas. She was explaining that Peter had no plan of getting an apartment with me, or of being in a relationship. His mother was trying to make me understand, to break the news to me. I had followed Peter from New Mexico to Edwards, Colorado, from Edwards to Dallas, and he never had any intention of being in a relationship with me. This wasn't Peter sitting across from me, this was his mother. He couldn't even be man enough to explain this to me himself. It was cool for me to be with him when I paid for everything, but when he didn't need me to pay, I wasn't invited anymore.

I had a small child, and all Peter wanted to do was party and have a good time. He wasn't ready to be in a committed relationship. His mother apologized and asked if she could help me get settled. She thought I should find something close to her home, so she could look out for me. She acknowledged I would never even be in Dallas if it weren't for her son. This was the most decisive warning I received early on, when I moved from Edwards, Colorado to Dallas, Texas.

I did as Peter's mom recommended, and found an apartment close to her home. She never visited me once. Felipe and I were on our own in an apartment in a city I didn't know. Peter would hang around when he pleased. He lived with his mom and step-dad with no responsibility. It was perfect for him. He would go out with friends, party, have fun, come home and sleep it off, hang out by the pool and then repeat the cycle the next night. He would stop by my place, have sex and continue on – no job, no stress, no worries.

It didn't take long before I had enough of Dallas. The shopping, heat and concrete were not for me. I moved back to New Mexico, leaving Dallas and Peter behind. I had lasted in an apartment on my own with Felipe, in Dallas, from April to July. I was back in New Mexico, living with Luna in Taos, by July 4th. Peter had promised he would come too. He said he couldn't stand Dallas and living with his parents. He couldn't wait to get back to New Mexico and the freedom it offered. I was to move first and he would follow in a couple of weeks and get his own place. Empty promises, nothing more, to free him of his guilt and sense of responsibility for what I was experiencing.

I moved to Taos and Peter got his own place, a studio apartment, in downtown Dallas shortly after I left. He partied all the time, got into drunken fights and acted like a teenager. I had a young son and Peter never wanted to grow up. We lived in different realities. My sense of self-worth was slipping with each promise not kept. I tried to get my bearings. I returned to my point of reference, to a place of strength, to Taos. I did all I could to keep myself from slipping back into old patterns.

I had helped Peter get a job as a web designer a few weeks after I moved to Dallas with him. That was how he was able to get the studio apartment after I moved back to Taos with Luna. That was how he had the money to travel to New York City for his friend's wedding that day. I went to the interview and pretended to be his agent. Peter made business cards for me to make the illusion seem real. He would completely freeze in interviews, suffering from panic attacks. He had never had a real job before, Monday through Friday, nine to five.

A short time after being back in New Mexico, I was back on top of the world. I was eating apricots, plums and apples from the orchard in the backyard. Living in the mountains, driving on dirt roads, enjoying all the comforts of a small artist community. Luna and her family had lived there for generations. When she was a child, the mail was delivered by horse and buggy and Luna would have to go outside and chop coal to heat her family home. It was not until after Marcos had passed that Luna had her grandmother's home converted from wood-burning stoves to gas heaters. Life was a blessing, and I was living in gratitude. I was in harmony with nature and myself. My self-esteem and confidence appeared to have returned to the surface.

Despite my joy, freedom and independence, something was missing. I didn't feel whole. I reached out to Peter and continued to maintain my connection with him. I made myself believe he would pull it together, stop partying and leave Dallas. I kept the relationship going as a long-distance friendship, in hopes of something more. I kept calling, writing and sending gifts from New Mexico. I was happy living with Luna and Felipe in Taos; other than my family, Peter was the only person I could share my happiness with. He was happy to listen to my adventures and be a friend; it had no impact on his freedom or responsibility.

I had created a wonderful world in Taos with Felipe and Luna. Luna and I would stay up late talking, sharing stories of Marcos and the family, and realizing how alike she and I were, as Marcos had always said. I truly came to love her. She has been a wonderful friend, and a reminder to me to be strong as a woman and a mom. She is the foundation that has made New Mexico home for me for all these years.

Married Again

On September 26, 1998, a month after my positive pregnancy test, I married Peter, in Las Vegas, Nevada, at The Wedding Chapel. My mom came to the wedding, along with Peter's mom and step-dad and a few of Peter's friends. On our wedding night, Peter went out with his friends, a bachelor party a day late. He came back to the room drunk and he passed out, lying sideways across the top of the blankets. I had stayed in the hotel room alone. Luna had stayed in Taos with Felipe. My mom was respecting the space, which should have been my wedding night. I ate my dinner alone in the restaurant of the hotel and went to bed by myself.

We drove back to Taos after the wedding in a rental car. My mom said, "You and Felipe had better go back to Dallas with Peter. It's not good to be married and live in separate states until he can move back to New Mexico." We drove my mom back to the airport in Albuquerque. Felipe and I packed our belongings, loaded up the rental car we had driven back from Las Vegas, and my SUV. Peter drove the rental car. Felipe and I drove in my SUV. We moved everything into Peter's studio apartment in Dallas, Texas. The apartment wasn't even a one bedroom. It could not have been more than 450 square feet. We had no chance of fitting everything into the apartment. Peter's brother moved out of his apartment and gave it to us. He found a new place closer to where his daughter lived with her mom in Plano, Texas. We were married, living in Dallas, and I was pregnant.

By October I had completely lost my direction again. I had become separated from myself, unable to find my path. I had absorbed another man's life. I gave up my own roots, the foundation that made me happy. What I wanted and needed had slipped through my fingers. I thought it was Dallas that overwhelmed me; it was not. It was my not being true to myself that overwhelmed me, not following my internal compass. My love and need of nature was left behind, neglected and unfulfilled. I had no trees, no Earth, no animals. No hikes in the mountains to help me find my direction. The warmth of the sun was removed from my skin. Happiness, freedom and a life lived on purpose eluded me.

My Social Security benefits went away when I married Peter; only Felipe received benefits now. There was less money coming in to live on, and my savings had been significantly depleted since I met Peter. I had purchased a trailer for cash when we moved to Edwards, and I was waiting for it to sell to recoup some of my losses. Peter still had the web-design job that I helped him get before I left Dallas the first time. At least this time he had some money coming in.

Here I was, pregnant, my nerves shot, living in Dallas again. The first time I lasted four months. I was constantly stressed. The tension I held in my stomach was unbearable. Then one day I went to the grocery store and pooped my pants. I couldn't hold it in as I raced to the bathroom. I was mortified. I couldn't help myself. I wasn't sick – my root, my connection to the Earth, who I was, had dropped out once again. It was different this time. There was no initial lightning strike to break me on the spot, no trauma or tragedy. I was being broken slowly without a sound.

I couldn't recognize my pattern. I didn't understand my experience, what was happening to me. My stomach was a nervous wreck every time I stepped out the door. I couldn't go anywhere without having to use the bathroom, and most of the time I didn't make it. I was pregnant, worried about getting the nutrients I needed, as the food raced out of my body. I went to an acupuncturist who did her best to help. I had several sessions with her that did seem to help. She taught me techniques to deal with the mounting tension, all the emotions that flooded me upon leaving the house. When I would get nervous, I was to press certain points to help me calm down. The acupuncturist had taped small ball bearings to the locations I needed to press to act like acupressure I was to use on myself.

My efforts to calm my stress were in vain. Peter quit his job as a web designer two weeks before Indigo was born, dreaming of creating his own web-design company. Peter never worked a regular job again. He sat in front of his computer screen at home exploring the world within, creating one company after another. I paid all the expenses of launching his new business ideas. He would pick up a few intermittent web jobs here and there – enough for him to buy a new snowboard, a skateboard, new clothes, restaurant meals. Stress and financial burdens were mounting by the day. Money was flowing out and nothing was coming in. My confrontations with him about money fell on deaf ears. His parents had nagged him for years about getting a job and being responsible. It meant nothing to him. He tuned me out just as he had his parents.

The storm was at my door. It couldn't get my attention, no matter how loud the winds howled. No need for action welled within me. No response to the warnings; the change in atmospheric pressure never signaled me to press for a new direction. I turned it all inward, my body riddled with the stress and tension. I made myself believe this was an everyday storm, not large enough to cause panic and fear – not enough to make me take notice, to bolt into action to maintain my survival. I was firmly held in the grasp of denial once more.

Indigo Born

Indigo was born at home, as I lay on a futon bed, in April of 1999. After my experience with Felipe I was adamant I would not have another hospital delivery. She was born in forty-five minutes, from first contraction to birth, with two mid-wives on hand to deliver her in my own home. Peter's mom and stepdad arrived shortly afterward to welcome her. Once she was born and I was cleaned up, I was up and walking freely about our apartment. She lay in the bassinet beside our bed – and I realized there was no pain, no hardship, no drama – and my body was strong, without any discomfort. I was thankful that I'd held to what I wanted for my experience, without compromise, and without listening to the fears of anyone else. I knew I was strong enough, capable of delivering a child at home, and I did.

That May, after Indigo was born, I received a Gerber daisy on Mother's Day and some chocolate-covered macadamia nuts. These were the first gifts Peter had ever given me. All his money was usually saved for what he wanted, yet this time he gave me something. I had some hope that things would be different, in anticipation of a beautiful new beginning.

I was certain the storm was not for me, that it would pass by without complaint.

My marriage to Peter was a constant series of moves, every four months. Peter and I moved from Dallas, a month after Indigo's birth, back to Albuquerque, New Mexico. From Albuquerque we moved to San Diego, California. We left San Diego and moved back to Dallas; from Dallas we moved to Austin, Texas. It took us exactly four months each time to realize the move hadn't changed what we were experiencing. I bought into the belief that it would be better each time.

We couldn't run fast enough to get away from our financial troubles and stress. Happiness had become a material possession to be acquired, an experience to be found. Lost was the joy welling within my heart. I had traded peace of mind and contentment for glitter. I looked to the promise of baubles offered, placing hope in a false future – a future dreamed of without consideration for responsibility.

We lived on Felipe's Social Security money, the last of my savings from the life insurance money I'd received when Marcos passed and the sale of the trailer in Edwards, Colorado. When that was gone, we moved on to my credit cards. Everything was in my name. I carried the burden; all the responsibility was on my shoulders – raising kids, doing chores and housework, paying bills, organizing and packing the moves. Peter remained on his computer, aloof in his own world.

I kept spending, trying to buy security, peace, happiness; the slightest sense of purpose and value in life. We would take trips to escape the overwhelming responsibility, come back and decide to move to where we had just visited. We were happy for that moment. Peter would say that it would be better there. I would believe him. We would move, to try and recreate what we had found in that small moment in time. It never lasted; nothing changed. I kept spinning, in constant motion, racing to keep up with all that needed to be done, from trips, to moves, to everyday errands.

I was exhausted, incapable of stopping and observing. There was no time or opportunity for making friends, allowing an outside voice to observe what was happening to me. I had no witness, within or outside of me. I was alone, racing to keep up. I never stopped to see that I was the only one racing, working, carrying the load. Peter played at his computer; when he was tired of that he would want to go on an adventure, go shopping, eat out – and I made it happen.

I was out of money, out of energy, drained and frustrated. It was a struggle at times to put food on the table. We were always hopeful, full of optimism that things would be different. Peter always had some new dream that he thought would make him rich. Each new move promised escape from this reality. It never came. We continued to spiral downwards, racing to unleash the storm that hovered without mercy. I couldn't compel the storm to release its torrent, no matter how furiously I pursued. I could never move fast enough to force the shift before its time. The storm was gathering its energy, the fury building within. It would come when it had ripened to a velocity, an intensity that I could not yet anticipate.

Chapter 13

World Trade Center

When we left Dallas and moved to Austin, we were living with a friend of Peter's from college. He was going to move out of his rental house, and we were going to move in. We stored most of our belongings in his garage until he moved out. We moved what we could fit into his two-bedroom house, until he was ready to move out.

I had dropped Felipe off at kindergarten and had returned home. When I stepped in the door, our roommate West hollered from the back room for me to turn on the TV. His new girlfriend, who had just been in town for a visit, was living in New York City. She was on the phone with West, frantic, asking him to find out what was happening. The building next door to where she worked was on fire.

I turned on the TV and began to watch the burning building, live on TV. I began relaying the information to West, that the building had been hit by an airplane and that she should get out of the area; the fire looked bad and was in the middle of the building. She worked in a high-security building, with a lot of rap recording artists, where all of the guards were heavily armed. On a good day, her office was a tense place to be – and with this situation next door, it was best to be gone. She was escorted out of the building, and she headed home immediately.

I continued to watch and listen to the reports, as West stayed on the phone with his girlfriend as she traveled to safety. I watched and listened to the reporter question what we were seeing live, as the second plane began to approach. It was beyond comprehension, our minds insisting it had to be an accident. The second plane crashed into the second World Trade Center tower. I screamed for Peter to wake up. He had to come see what was happening.

I watched for hours, my eyes fixed to the screen, the buildings ablaze. People jumping, falling from the floors above, trapped in the fiery inferno. Reports of all planes being grounded, all travel stopped. Fear building, the unknown and unfathomable, unfolding in real time. All I could think was, where's Katelyn?

A third plane, now off course, heading for the Pentagon, and another crash. It was surreal. I pulled myself away from the screen and raced, with other parents, frantically trying to find my child. I had to get Felipe from his kindergarten class and bring him home. The need for everyone to be together, to be prepared, was pressing upon me. I found Felipe and immediately returned home. Not long after, I watched as the first of the Twin Towers fell to the ground, and then the second. It was impossible to grasp the magnitude of the fear and loss of life happening, as we all gathered around the small TV screen.

When I saw the second plane hit, and understood the beginning of what was happening, I began frantically calling my sister. She lived in New York City and worked downtown, a couple of blocks away from the Twin Towers. All circuits were busy. There was no way to reach her on her cell phone. Every phone in New York City was desperately seeking connection, loading the circuits beyond capacity.

Katelyn had always been a survivor. I knew in my heart that she would be watching, paying attention and making decisions. That's just who she was. By evening I was able to connect with her for a few brief moments by phone. My beliefs were confirmed. She was the smartest, strongest woman I knew. She had been in the warehouse of her office, even further downtown, when it had happened. She saw the smoke and the people beginning to run toward her. She immediately found an ATM, grabbed as much cash as she could from her account and began running uptown in her five-inch heels and high-end dress clothes with the crowds of people flooding out of lower Manhattan. The financial district was evacuating.

She watched the storefronts as she passed. Racing by, she saw one that sold running shoes and apparel. She ran inside, bought tennis shoes and running clothes with the cash she had in hand. She changed her clothes and began to run. She made it on foot out of New York City, across the bridge, all the way back home to her apartment in Brooklyn. She was fine, she was safe, she was alive. She kept her wits about her, reacted immediately without hesitation and took the action required to get herself to safety. How could I expect anything less from Katelyn?

Life and death became real for me again that day, and in the days that followed. The devastation of the World Trade Center created a storm big enough to break through to me. It allowed me to pause, to feel, to look up and see that I was lost, that I needed to take action once more. I felt myself return and connect through the raw emotions poured out on the TV screen. I couldn't leave. I sat there and experienced it all, connecting with my own lost emotions of shock, fear, heartache and loss. I felt all that I had repressed, pushed down within me. My heart broke open, sharing in the suffering and pain I witnessed. I was done. I was broken. I had had enough. I made a choice, stood up and took action. I decided we were leaving. I took the lead. We were going back to Taos. I was going to live with Luna and figure this out.

I would study Kundalini Yoga, and live a simple life in a small, forgotten town, off the radar, out of sight of the world. There was a center for Kundalini Yoga in Taos. I could study to become an instructor. I would create a life of value and service. I was not going to follow Peter on his whims, without choice, without responsibility any longer. I was going to create the life I wanted to live, filled with meaning and purpose, living in service from my heart. Peter was adamant that he was coming with me.

The Christmas Gifts

We were to leave Austin, Texas and go back to Taos, New Mexico just before Christmas 2001. We celebrated an early Christmas with Peter's family. We were to drive the U-Haul from Dallas, as it was cheaper to get in Dallas than in Austin. I had no money. My mother, as a gift, was going to pay for the U-Haul. When she tried to pay with her credit card they wouldn't let her, as she would not be driving the vehicle.

We asked Peter's mom to help, explaining the situation. She told me to call my seventy-year-old grandparents and ask them to pay. I come from poor, simple, country folk in upstate New York who do not have a lot of money. The jobs are low paying, the economy in shambles, the communities poverty stricken. They had no money to help me pay for the U-Haul. I was humiliated. Peter's mom and step-dad listened, standing beside me, while I made the call to my grandparents, begging for money they didn't have to give.

Peter's mom told me to return the gifts that they had given me the night before; that was my only choice. She said, "You should have asked for what you needed for Christmas, and not accepted gifts." She was trying to teach me to take responsibility, accountability for my actions. I drove to the store and tried to return my gift cards. Gift cards couldn't be returned or traded for cash at TJ Maxx and Ross. I was running out of time; I had to pick up the U-Haul. I was frantic.

Peter's mom relented, saying, "I will buy the gift cards from you." The very ones she had given me as a Christmas gift. I asked that some of Peter's gifts, clothes she had gone shopping with him to buy, be returned. She said no, they fit him nicely and he had already been wearing some of them. They couldn't be returned. It was all on me to support her son. I was broken, left kneeling at her feet, begging for mercy for her to help me protect her son and granddaughter. I had no value. I was humiliated and broken. I did what was necessary to get back to Luna and the security of Taos. I had terminated our lease in Austin. I was cornered and desperate. I was willing to endure the humiliation to gain freedom.

The drive back to Taos was exhausting. I packed the whole house myself, as I had every single time we moved. Peter would pack his computer and personal items only. I then carried everything to the truck. He would stay inside and organize the boxes and furniture, so nothing would fall. For every move, we did this exact same routine. I would plan, prepare and carry the load.

Peter would hang out in the truck and wait for me to carry all of the boxes, and clean the house so we could get on the road. He would drive the U-Haul. I would follow behind in my SUV, completely drained from all the effort to get out the door. He would drive in the fast lane the entire time. I could never get him to understand that it was a passing lane only, that it was inconsiderate to travel in that lane going slow in a moving truck.

We made it back to Taos. Coming up over the ridge, my body fell apart. I was exhausted, relieved to be back home on familiar terrain, where I knew I could find my strength. I had to pull over and throw up repeatedly at the rest stop, at the crest of the mountain, where the expanse opens and you can see the Taos Gorge. My head was pounding with a migraine. I could no longer function by the time we arrived on Christmas Eve at midnight on Luna's doorstep. My wounds were fresh from the experience with Peter's mom.

I asked Peter to bring in my plants; they meant the world to me. He didn't, and they all froze in the back of the U-Haul that night. I wouldn't let them die. They were a part of me, a symbol of my own survival. I brought them into the house the next morning and nursed them back from death. Some only had one leaf remaining, from once-grand, robust plants. I saved them, as I would save myself. These plants sit beside me now, again fertile, strong and robust. They are my witness; they remind me daily of my survival and who I have become.

Chapter 14

Alchemy

When we left Austin, and planned to move back to Taos, I was the reason. I had purchased a Kundalini video at Whole Foods Market and fallen in love with the experience and possibility of becoming a Kundalini yoga instructor. There was a Kundalini Center in Taos. In my plan, I would move to Taos, go to the yoga studio to meet the Kundalini instructor I had contacted online and become an instructor.

I was set on learning the skills I needed to be free once and for all from the lack of self-esteem and confidence that had driven me to live my life through others, to express myself as a victim. The first week we arrived in Taos, I made arrangements to meet the instructor. I had directions to the studio; it was easy to find. Peter insisted that he would come too. If I might find an opportunity to create for myself, he would find a way to make it work for him too. Since Peter was coming and Luna was at work, I had to bring the whole family with me to meet the instructor.

Peter, the kids and I were crammed in the small waiting room, at the Kundalini Center, when the most unusual man sat down. He was dressed in a long-sleeved black shirt and black cotton pants. He wore a large, Australian, wide-brimmed black-leather hat with two leather tassels that hung in the back. I had seen him riding his bike along the side of the road, as we drove up to the yoga studio. For some reason his riding – the pace, the rhythm – had reminded me of *The Wizard of Oz*. When the tornado hit, the wicked woman who came to take Toto away from the farm – who later became the wicked witch's sister – was pedaling her bike in the midst of the storm as though nothing were happening. That was exactly how he appeared to me with his big leather hat, pedaling his bike. He was somehow different from everyone else.

Now I was sitting across from this man in the small waiting area at the Kundalini Yoga studio. He began talking about Alchemy, a system he had created and taught in a class outside in a park on Saturdays. He was a Lama, among other titles, who had traveled the world studying various disciplines of spiritual practice. I asked where I would find the park where he taught his class. He told me the name; I didn't recognize it, but I had a sense immediately of exactly where the park was.

This was my new beginning. I dropped the idea of studying Kundalini yoga and committed to studying this new system of Alchemy. I continued on to meet with the yoga instructor, who was a Sikh, as planned. I attended one class under him. I enjoyed it, but it wasn't like my video at all. I felt disillusioned by my initial desire to pursue Kundalini yoga. My intent had waned in comparison to the mystery and intrigue I felt sitting in the waiting room that day, when the Lama had shared his system of Alchemy.

The yoga instructor warned me, saying, "His methods are not safe. He's too extreme. It's dangerous to study with this man. His practices could kill a person. The energy he works with is too intense, and this is not a good path to follow." I didn't listen. I took his reaction and warnings as a form of jealousy, an extreme response due to his not wanting to lose me as a paying student. I should have listened, and not assumed I knew what motivated him to speak out.

The next Saturday I got dressed, ate a full breakfast of pancakes, and went to find the park to attend my first class. My stomach was a nervous ball of energy in anticipation. New situations always stressed me out. Being on time, finding the park, meeting new people, all mixed with Peter's lackadaisical attitude which had caused us to arrive late, sent me into a frenzy of nervous tension. Peter had no intention of missing out; he had to be there. He had no interest in taking Kundalini yoga with me, but if this was a mysterious man, claiming to possess powerful energy, he was going to be a part of it.

Peter always needed to be special in some way. He was drawn to anyone who claimed to have special gifts of intuition or knowing of any kind. He was interested in the metaphysical, not for personal growth, resolving old issues or forgiving himself and others. He wanted power, gifts and special abilities instead. In his eyes, the important spiritual teachers and gurus had such abilities. He wanted to be like them. He wanted to be a teacher and have people following him who thought he was important. Or if not the teacher, then he wanted to be closely associated with the teacher, so that he could still enjoy the perks of superiority.

Peter wanted to be famous. He made a point of telling people his birthday was two days before Clint Eastwood's. In hindsight I realize this was to compensate for his panic attacks and his inability to cope with stressful situations where he had to be accountable, such as job interviews. This was why he never had a real job, except for the one I interviewed with him for, acting as his agent. Like a kid, Peter wanted to be a superhero to make up for feeling small, inadequate and without power.

It was a cold January day. Felipe and Indigo stayed home with Luna, while Peter and I left to attend the class outside. I never liked to be out in the cold. I had poor circulation, causing my hands and feet to freeze and get frostbite if I wasn't careful. We pulled into the park on a dirt driveway. There were tennis courts on the right-hand side, just off the parking area. We pulled up and parked in front of the tennis courts. I watched for a moment from the safety of my seat, before climbing out of the Vanagon. I had to pause, let my stomach settle. If I moved too quickly and didn't dissipate the energy, I would have to run to the bathroom.

I seldom made it to the bathroom in time in those situations. I would soil my underpants on the way. Mortified, I would have to adapt, adjust, so no one would ever suspect. I carried extra underwear in my purse and wore maxi pads in new situations, so that I would be prepared for the worst-case scenario. I did everything I could to be in control of the uncontrollable.

The problem was that I was never in control; Peter was. The monkey-minded one – with no plan, no cares and no worries – was in control. What I didn't understand at the time was that it was all a façade. He was pretending to be carefree and not worried, when in fact he was scared out of his mind. His pretending not to care gave him the ability to feel superior, to laugh at me for my nervousness and my weakness in soiling my pants. It allowed him to make me the butt of the joke for my honesty about how I was feeling.

As I sat in the Vanagon, I quickly scanned my surroundings. The outhouse was on the other side of the class. There would be no discreet way of getting there, without disrupting the class. That's why I always arrived early for new situations. It allowed me time to settle, get my bearings, use the bathroom and get a feel for the people who were present. It allowed me to integrate at my own pace into the environment. These have always been the necessary steps and precautions that I've had to take to ground and protect myself.

I have always been prone to nervousness, yes. What was really happening in these situations with Peter was that I was picking up his hidden nervous energy and his fear of not being accepted. That was what was pushing me over the edge – not my own small amount of nervousness. I was made to believe that it was all me. That it was all in my head. That I was weak and out of control. This was not true. I discovered that I am an empath. I feel the world around me to such a degree it can be difficult at times to separate myself from the flood of emotions that penetrates my being, like hearing all stations on the radio at the same time.

I didn't realize I had been picking up other people's emotions, as an empath, for a long time. I believed what I was told since childhood – that it was all in my head, that it was my fear and weakness. I was told I needed to get control of myself. It was never true. I am overwhelmed by the emotions of others near me, or those that I care about, whether they are close by or on another continent. New situations always involve other people – that's why I would get all out of sorts, my bearings lost. I needed time to adjust to the new energies as they flooded into my emotional centers.

It took me years to understand that I pick up all the nervous tension in a space and feel it as my own. I would be fine, not nervous at all, knowing where I was going and not worried about attending the event. Then I would pull up to the event, pause in my car and feel it all. I could feel the emotions before I even stepped out of the car or entered the event. My stomach would twist in knots of nervous tension. I would talk to myself and ask what's going on. I would tell myself that I'm fine. I'm not afraid. I'm not stressed. Where's this coming from? I began to observe others coming and going, and I realized I was feeling them, all of them. I could sense the tension from those setting up the event and those attending. I could watch and feel the ones emitting the most unresolved energy out into the environment.

I am fine when I am at home or alone out in the woods, far from people. Those I encounter while in nature I can handle, as I am able to pull up the energy of the Earth at the moment of contact. I do not encounter people without being grounded in my environment, unless it is a new situation or a surprise. I made the connection and became aware, accepting who I am on all levels. I have to consciously draw my awareness to my own feelings and segregate them from the total of my experience. I have learned, as time passed, to create a shield, a merkaba, to protect myself from picking up these out-of-balance energies.

Peter knew that arriving late would put me at a disadvantage. It's almost as if that's what he needed, so he would stand out and no one would notice me. He needed to be the center of attention – even though this was my plan, my idea and my intention for creating a life for myself. As I would pull back and hide, having not been able to control my arrival or preparation, he would step forward as the class clown, drawing attention to himself as the person who arrived late. That was the absolute last thing I ever wanted – people's eyes on me for not being responsible or respectful enough to arrive on time and not having time to prepare myself.

After pausing as long as I could, I climbed out of the car and we both found our places at the back, as the class had already begun. There were maybe fifteen people standing in three lines between a small covered park bench on a concrete slab and the tennis courts. A large cottonwood tree stood sentinel over the bench. The outhouse was at the far end, equidistant between the tennis courts and the bench. I stood in the back facing the outhouse.

Leaving My Body

Class began with the first of the Five Elements – the Jongs of Maoshan. The posture was to be held for seven to ten minutes. I held I-Jong, the first posture, for three minutes before I began to feel lightheaded. I knew this feeling well, and I knew I didn't have much time to get myself seated before I would black out. I was sweating and seeing stars – the last signs before my hearing would go and I would experience a complete blackout – and then find myself waking up on the ground.

I made my way to the park bench, reaching for the table to guide me into place. Sitting down usually stopped me from fainting, but not this time. I began to watch my surroundings dim, then fade away. The sparkles of bright light increased in my vision as my consciousness faded, the sound of the void enveloping me. That was it. I was out – gone completely. I could see myself clearly. I was back home in Luna's house, in the warmth and safety of my own bed. I was editing out this moment in the park from my awareness. In reality, I had never passed out before and seen myself in my unconscious state, let alone seeing my body in a different location than the one where I had passed out.

Just as quickly as I had left consciousness, I was being pulled back to this moment. I could feel someone trying to lift me up and out of bed. I tried to stop them in my mind, as I became aware of the smell of the mud my face was pressed into and the voices of concerned students nearby. I was returning to the park I had left only moments before. I was regaining consciousness. I was aware that I had passed out and that people were around me, trying to get me back on the bench. I was lost in the void, surrounded in black; my vision had not returned.

I could feel myself being picked up from the ground, being pushed into an upright position, sitting on the bench. I was conscious now; my awareness had returned – but everything was still black. My eyes were open and I was in darkness. I was not afraid. I was at peace, calm, smiling and sitting on the bench. My body was on fire, burning hot, my mouth parched, as if I had been in the desert for days. I felt as if steam was rising up and out from the top my head, escaping through my clothes and out at my collar. I was wet, my body moist with sweat.

The Lama was next to me, sitting on the bench. I could hear him give instructions for the class to return to holding the postures. I was desperate for a drink. I was blind, and all I could think about was water. I begged the Lama, "Please, can I have a drink of water?" He told me, "Not yet; your body temperature is still too high. The hot tea I have with me could shock your system. You have to cool down first." On this cold winter day, sitting outside in the park, I was too hot to drink tea, cooled in a thermos, for fear of overheating my system.

I was always cold. At this moment I was on fire. I felt as if I was going to die of thirst, literally. This was the closest I have ever felt to pure panic that I couldn't get water. I have never been that thirsty in my entire life. I tried to focus on something else, not think about my deep need for water. I barely gave more than a passing thought to the fact that I still couldn't see, that I had no vision at all. I was sitting in darkness, next to a virtual stranger, in a park I had never been to before, surrounded by people I had never met – and all I could think about was getting a sip of water. I had come late; no one here except for Peter even knew who I was. Of course, at this moment when I needed him, Peter was nowhere to be found. He had gone back to class with the other students, probably pretending he didn't know me. At this point I didn't care – all I wanted was water.

Finally, I had cooled enough. I don't know how long it took, as I had no concept of time or space; all I knew was that I was being poured a small cup of tea, and soon I could drink. I sipped the hot tea from the tiny cup, the lid of the thermos the Lama had brought with him. He warned me to drink slowly, not too much or too fast, or I could go into shock. I was completely calm, with no worries, no stress, no regard for my continued loss of vision. I sipped the tea, a thimble in the vastness of my thirst, and waited for more to come as he refilled my cup.

My nervousness over the first class and a new environment was gone. I was sitting on the bench completely blind, having passed out after the first three minutes of class. I was relaxed through every cell of my being, as I had not been in years. Instead of my usual way of feeling in a situation like this, filled with humiliation and terror, I was feeling calm, peaceful and happy for no reason. I felt as if I were sitting in a meadow surrounded by flowers in the warm sunlight. I was in a beautiful place in my mind.

Eventually, my body had cooled all the way to being chilled, as the sweat on my body began to freeze in the below-freezing temperature outside. I remained seated on the bench, now alone. I could hear the class carry on. Everyone continued as they had before I passed out. I struggled to see a glimpse of the world around me, and at first nothing emerged – until, slowly, I began to see the faintest orange outline of a human being. It was a young man in front of me, holding one of the Jong postures. I could make out his aura, the faint glow surrounding his body. I shouted with joy, "I can see. I can see an orange glow outlining someone."

I focused on the glowing image, as it slowly began to take shape and form into a human being. I was regaining my sight. I was sitting on a park bench, and once more, my life had changed forever. I felt completely different. I was happy, my body at rest, no longer in a constant state of racing. I was witnessing, observing, without the constant influx of thoughts, worries or fears. The relentless voice in my head, feeding my insecurities and self-consciousness, was silent. My focus had shifted to the basics of survival: water, vision, consciousness. At the same moment I was at peace, life was no longer complicated and overwhelming.

The class gathered around the table for a break, and a gentle woman in her mid-forties reached toward my face, saying, "Oh dear, let me brush the mud off your face." I had fallen, just missing the concrete corner of the cement patio under the bench. Peter had returned with the group of students now on break and asked the Lama, "Why did you let her fall? Why did you leave her?" The Lama replied, "I needed to know which direction she would fall." I fell forward and slightly to the side, an indication that I was ready to surrender, ready to receive. It was time for my opening.

I noticed that Peter had not stayed by me, reassured me or cared for me after I passed out. Along with everybody else, he came to see me more out of curiosity. He went back to class when it resumed, while I sat on the bench struggling. He left me alone and blind on a park bench with strangers. He returned at the break with the rest of the class and acted as if he barely knew me. Peter would forever be concerned with his own needs. I never mattered to him.

Awakening

After class was over we left, returning to the mundane tasks of living. I didn't return as the same being. I continued to feel different than ever before, an intangible existence. I spent the rest of the day feeling as if I was phasing in and out of another reality, unified with the energy of life itself. I was ethereal. I felt as though I were walking in space, three feet above the ground, as if I were gliding. I could actually see a plane of existence that coexisted with our current reality. It was surreal. I was light, giddy, without tension, as if immersed in a pool of warm water. I had no concern for the pressures of life. I was purely an observer with no stake in the outcome. I felt the energy of loving kindness envelop me. I was free, in total acceptance of the world around me. I was transformed.

When I went to Walmart to get a gift for Felipe to attend a birthday party for a friend from school, I didn't feel the usual stress and tension, being in close proximity to so many people. I couldn't feel them at all. I was in a bubble of light, floating above this level of consciousness. I was a new being, an observer passing through, laughing and filled with gladness. I was unaffected by any of the hustle and bustle or need to decide what was the best gift to give. It was all good. There were no negative emotions within me. My face was stretched with a smile from ear to ear. I would break into laughter over the smallest thing. I felt a deep love for everything around me. The smells that had overwhelmed me in the past, emanating from those nearby, was gone. The darkness and harshness of the world was gone. It was all still present, but in my new reality, my new existence, it had no impact.

The Day After

By the next day, the effects had worn off, as if I had taken drugs only to return to who I had been upon sobering. I was back to my old self, only more vulnerable and raw than I'd been before. I felt sick, my body overwhelmed with the flu. I had a fever; my throat was sore and my voice hoarse. I called the Sikh from the Kundalini center and asked for medicine to help my body heal and purify itself from the event the day before. He came to Luna's house and brought me the medicine while I lay in bed. He had warned me, and I hadn't listened; now I was so sick I couldn't get out of bed. It took me nearly a week to regain enough strength and stamina to return to my daily routine.

Peter was back to his verbal abuse, and I had lost all hope. He hadn't experienced a thing at the class. The practices hadn't impacted him at all. I was still gripped by the effects. As my body overcame the sickness, I began feeling the extreme opposite emotions of what I had experienced on the day of the class with the Lama. I felt as though I was filled with all the negative emotions of the whole world, drowning my spirit in hopelessness. Now, instead of walking in a separate reality, in the world but not of it, I was in the world without hope, without love.

In my vulnerability, Peter continued to attack. He knew just what to say to destroy my spirit. I lay in bed, willing myself to die – my breathing slowing, my heart barely pumping. I was killing myself by the power of my own will. I was going within, turning out my own light. I couldn't do it anymore. The pain was too great; this reality of suffering without hope was too hard to bear. I was slipping away. The contrast I had experienced by moving from a world filled with beauty and joy – to one filled with suffering and anguish – was too much to bear. I couldn't assimilate the harshness, the truth of this contrast, into my being. The pain of my sickness and fever riddled my body. It was like experiencing heaven one day, only to be cast out the very next. I didn't want to live anymore.

At that very moment, when all hope was lost, an image of the Lama's face emerged before me. He was smiling at me, wearing his large-brimmed leather hat. I could feel love and compassion flowing from him into me. I smiled back. I couldn't continue slipping away. I stopped. I was back in my body. I couldn't smile and receive loving kindness, and also will myself to die. I chose to live – the compassion of a near-stranger ignited my will to live once more. I would survive this too. Love had entered where nothing else could, and healed my broken heart. I was shattering into light once more.

Act 4

Chapter 15

Bankruptcy

The gravity of my situation formed around me, as I was listening to Grammie speak on the other end of the phone while I sat on the couch in Luna's living room, "I understand that you want to pay the debt on your credit cards. But how much do you owe?" I responded, "Around $35,000." "How did you ever get that far into debt?" Grammie was appalled, her voice breaking into in her heavy Austrian accent, reserved for when she was really upset.

I defended my situation, "From all the moves, buying food, eating out, vacations, having two kids." She was getting mad now. "You had more than enough to take care of yourself and Felipe when Marcos died. That husband of yours really bugs me. He needs to do something to take care of you and the kids. I hate to say it, you know I would never, unless I believed the situation was that bad, but you need to file for bankruptcy."

I couldn't believe the words coming out of her mouth. My grandparents were frugal, responsible to a fault. She explained, "You have no money to pay back your debt; you owe too much to ever repay it. It will just keep growing, with interest. You have to file for bankruptcy and start over. You have no choice. I'm sorry, sweetie; you know I would never tell you this if it weren't true." If anyone else had presented this to me I would have said no. I would have argued, stood on principle, fought back. Not with Grammie. She never took the moral high ground with me. If she was saying it, it was true. I relented, "I love you, Grammie. I agree, I have no choice. I will file for bankruptcy."

I hung up the phone, opened the phone book and began calling attorneys who advertised bankruptcy services. Grammie had assured me she would get Grandpa to help pay for the bankruptcy. The $1,000 fee would be paid in full from my grandparents' savings.

I found the attorney's office in a new contemporary building, away from the main road. The receptionist had an authenticity about her that was refreshing. Lush green plants hung over the edge of her desk, bringing life into the drudgery of law. She guided Peter and me to the attorney's office. The attorney had created a pleasant, bright and lovely work space, filled with paintings of aspen trees. As we entered, I commented on how beautiful her paintings were; she explained that her husband was the artist, well known locally. She stood and introduced herself, shaking our hands, making us feel welcome. She offered us a seat and asked if we would like anything to drink. I said "No, thank you." Peter said, "Sure, I'll have a cup of coffee." The receptionist quickly disappeared, then returned with Peter's coffee.

I felt comforted, reassured by her calm demeanor. She was tall, slender and beautiful. Her appearance was professional in every way. Her voice was gentle, her eyes were kind, conveying compassion and understanding. She had the bankruptcy paperwork laid out before her on the desk. As she began filling out the first lines, she looked up at us briefly and asked, "Will both of your names be on the filing?" It was less of a question than a confirmation. I said "Yes." Peter said, "No, do it in her name, it was her credit cards."

I broke, to hear those words out loud. I began to cry, tears streaming down my cheeks, dripping down my neck. "In my name," my mind was racing, no consequences, no responsibility for Peter Pan, no impact on his life, his credit. It was all my money – my savings and then my credit. All used to buy happiness he was incapable of maintaining. I gasped, trying to catch my breath, as the tears stained my face with mascara. Right there in the attorney's office, in front of this kind, caring, professional woman. I couldn't hold it in any longer. The pain, the desperation, all the fear I had been holding, welling within me, flooded out – the embarrassment of his words and actions hitting me in the face.

The storm had begun. It had waited, holding its course, hovering above for so long I had forgotten. The winds were whipping, full force, the hail pelting me in the face. The cold freezing me to my core. My heart shocked by its arrival. I had endured, waiting, begging for the storm to come, pursuing its release. I had given up hope, forgotten its presence. It was upon me, ripping me apart, allowing me to feel through the numbness I had survived. All while sitting in this lovely, serene office filled with beauty and kindness.

My denial was shattering. I looked in the face of truth and accepted it. I said "No. No, it will be in both our names. I am not doing this alone." The attorney looked at me, saying nothing. She saw it all in that one moment, as he tried shifting it all on me, like the Christmas gifts I'd had to return mere weeks before. That was it. I stood up. I would no longer carry the load for him. We filed jointly for bankruptcy.

Our Volkswagen Vanagon was repossessed. I knew it would be. I cleaned out all of our personal items, removed the car seats and left it ready for repossession. One morning I woke up and it was gone. Peter made a deal with one of his brothers and got a very used VW Rabbit. It was a stick shift. I didn't know how to drive a stick. Peter spent a day in a parking lot teaching me, and that was it. I had errands to run, responsibilities. I had to learn, so I did my best. Small towns are kind to such ignorance. I got where I needed to go; other drivers endured it with laughter and shaking their heads.

I got a job in an art gallery and worked to pay the bills. Peter stayed at home and continued doing what he always did: working on the computer, creating businesses that never existed, dreaming up ideas for work he never followed through on. He made web designs, logos, everything – yet no income ever came. I worked, did the cooking, took care of the kids. Luna did not like this one bit, but she held her tongue, not wanting to interfere and hoping I would figure this out.

Our bankruptcy was officially filed by the United States Bankruptcy Court District of New Mexico on April 2, 2002, the sixth anniversary of Marcos' passing. Our hearing had been in Santa Fe. We sat in front of the woman who handled the case. Every single item we owned had been listed and submitted before the bankruptcy court. I had created the list, marking every item as requested.

The woman handling our case asked about my butterflies – one for my graduation, the other for the birth of Indigo. Both had been gifts from my sister. She had mercy on me, realizing I hadn't bought them myself, and she let me keep them. I was the only one ever asked to give anything up, or have something taken away. Peter was never held accountable by anyone. I was the one held accountable, the one who had to pay the price.

After the bankruptcy was awarded, we were officially free of our debt. Immediately following our hearing Peter said, "Let's go out for lunch and celebrate." I couldn't believe it. He tried to justify getting his way, saying that this is why they grant you a bankruptcy, so your money will flow back into the economy. It was bullshit. This was wrong. You don't celebrate not having to pay back what you owe, what you borrowed in good faith.

I kept hoping that once the bankruptcy was done, and we no longer had debt over our heads, that things would get better. We would have fun and stop fighting about money. It never happened. Things didn't change or get better. My grandparents helped us buy a vehicle, giving us $5,000 from their savings to be paid back when we received our tax return.

Peter went to Dallas and picked out a used black Nissan Pathfinder, again a stick shift. He had gone to Dallas and picked it out without my input. He knew I struggled, and couldn't manage a stick shift, but he bought one anyway. It was a car he had wanted to buy since I met him in college, right down to the color black. He was a selfish person who had never been held accountable for his actions by anyone. He would never change. He was continually rewarded for his behavior. It was done. I could see that Peter was a con, a master manipulator. Finally, I was waking up. I went back to the same attorney, a few weeks after our bankruptcy was official, and filed for divorce. I had to get Peter to sign a release, so that she could represent me, as she had just represented both of us for bankruptcy.

File for Divorce

The first bills came in for my initial meeting with the attorney. It hit me, brought me to my knees. I couldn't afford to pay for the divorce. I was beside myself. I'd spent every penny I had on Peter. Now I needed money – my life and my children's lives depended on this need, and there was nothing left for me. I couldn't ask my family. They didn't have anything left to give.

The storm raged on; it would not be over quickly. I would have to hold on; keep moving, accepting and forgiving. I was adamant that this transformation would be permanent. That was why this storm was so different from the first. It stirred with warnings, marked its passage through time, and in the exact moment required, it poured forth.

The attorney told me about a women's shelter down the road that could help. I pulled up to the shelter and paused, witnessing the high-security measures in place to protect the women inside. I came through the security doors, buzzed in from the gate outside. I asked to speak with a counselor. I was led down a small corridor and was asked to sit in a chair beside a woman's desk.

The counselor was kind and patient, not pressing or in a hurry. She made me feel that she had all the time in the world to sit with me. That all she wanted was to listen to what I had to say. This moment was all about what *I* needed. She asked me what brought me here today, what was happening? She made sure I knew I wasn't alone, and I didn't need to be afraid that anyone would ever know I was here. Her questions didn't feel invasive. Everything about her told me she was genuine, trustworthy and compassionate. Her words emanated a true concern for my well-being, and a desire to fully understand what I was experiencing right now and help in any way she could.

I felt no judgment about my appearance, my age, or what might have brought me to this moment. I raised my voice to speak; it cracked, broke and gave way. I had found someone of mercy, speaking to me from the heart, and it shattered me. Her kindness broke me in half. I couldn't hold anything back. I had found the one person who was willing to see me, to hear me without judgment, the one who promised to help me figure this out. My story came flooding out in pieces, chunks of recollections, the warnings that I'd allowed to pass me by. My fears, my self-judgment, my lack of self-esteem and self-love rushed out of me. All of it, poured out onto the floor beneath our feet, sinking back into the Earth to be transformed into strength once more.

It wasn't my fault. I wasn't alone. This happened to more women than I could ever imagine. This was not the stigma of weak women. Strong, confident, successful women were not left untouched by this epidemic of abuse, this lack of self-worth and self-esteem. There was no outward sign that could define, pinpoint or reveal what any woman had experienced. Someone could pass any of us on the street and think us to be ordinary, going about our regular everyday lives as successful, happy people.

It hit me. I had allowed myself to become an abused woman. I had embraced the mind of a victim, who had no choice, no voice, no power, no confidence or self-esteem. It was real. The attorney was not advising me to come here just because I needed to get help paying her bills. She could see I needed help, an intervention, because I was an abused woman. I had been beaten down, my self-esteem destroyed, my money taken. I was given a witness, someone willing to step forward and intervene on my behalf, another woman who was not afraid to reach out and show me the way back to my strength within.

The fighting between Peter and me had ultimately escalated into a physical confrontation when there was no more money to be given. I was one of *those* women. The ones that are seen from the outside, whose actions cannot be fathomed. No one else would take what I did, not get out or stand up for themselves. From the outside, this is how judgment is passed. Like watching a horror film, "I would never be so stupid, so weak, so filled with fear, so foolish. I would call for help, get the car keys and leave. I wouldn't enter that dark room. I wouldn't go back to try and find one last sign of hope." Until a person is required to walk in another person's shoes, no one will ever know what might have or could have been done differently.

When our fighting escalated into a physical confrontation, I had asked Peter for receipts, from a supposed business trip to Dallas when he bought the Nissan Pathfinder, to use for tax purposes. He became angry and attacked me with his full power. I fought him off. Shaken and trembling, I ran outside. This was the first time he had physically attacked me. He knew it was over. He had no need for me any longer. Now that I had no money, I was garbage to be thrown away.

The storm was freeing me. It was pounding down on me once again, breaking me open, shattering me into being, releasing the light within me. This was the second pass after a brief calm following the bankruptcy. The calm that tricks you into believing the storm is over. Here I sat in a women's shelter, begging for money to be set free from Peter.

Once I had calmed, having purged my story and poured it forth for all to witness, the woman sitting beside me said, without hesitation, "We will pay for your divorce." She got me scheduled to receive group counseling, to help me heal and to learn the tools I needed to regain my power. She handed me a book, as I stood to walk out the door that day, saying, "Read this – it will help you understand what you have been through." I needed a guide so that I could be my own witness, moving forward. The tricks, the choices, the concessions made, can all be that elusive to one who is in the midst of the storm. The signs are obvious in retrospect. To the outside observer, though, it's bewildering that the victim doesn't understand – but that doesn't make it not so.

I was overwhelmed with gratitude. I would make it. I would be granted my freedom. I would learn how to stand up, have a voice, maintain my personal power, set boundaries and recognize when I was in danger. With the help, kindness and generosity of the shelter and the compassionate heart of a stranger, who listened without judgment to the voice of my soul, I was free. My divorce was finalized on February 12, 2003. I was pronounced divorced by the Eighth Judicial District, County of Taos, State of New Mexico. I was married on September 26, 1998 and survived to divorce him five years later.

I paid my grandparents my share of what we owed. Peter never repaid them. He took the car in the divorce and never paid me a cent. My friend Marie called from Texas. She and her friends were driving to meet me with a Toyota Corolla that I could have for free, and it was an automatic. I was elated. I had thought I was alone, that no one saw, no one cared, no one would help me. It was not true, and it never had been. They were all waiting for me to see, to make the shift that would allow them back into my life.

Chapter 16

Response to my Divorce

After all I had experienced, the extremes of life and death, I still decided that I wanted to study with the Lama. As I studied, practicing the arts, I became stronger each week. I was beginning to grow, to experience laughter and freedom once more. I was beginning my ascent from where I had been left on the ground, kneeling, begging Peter's mom for help. Slowly, over time, I was regaining my personal power, self-esteem and confidence. I soaked up the energy of Taos, the mountains, nature and the ancient practices. I was coming back into my own power. In the process of growing stronger, becoming empowered, I filed for bankruptcy and decided I would get a divorce. I had the support of Luna and other strong women at my side. Those who did not support me, I ignored.

In fact, many in my practice group were now friends with Peter and didn't support my decision to divorce him, as it was making them uncomfortable. They thought Peter was fun and that I had no real reason to divorce him. They began a small men-only group, including Peter while excluding me. This was a special group led by the Lama that I was not permitted to attend, being one of the few females studying with him. They learned many secret practices in this separate group that the women were not allowed to attend. This should have set off warning signals for me, but it didn't.

When I told the Lama of my decision, he neither encouraged nor discouraged me. He listened to me, and agreed that when he had found me I was like a dog that had crawled under the porch to die. My will to live was gone, and I was waiting for death. He was confident that he had worked with Peter, placing shields over him so he could never again cause me harm. He believed that Peter would not continue his abusive behavior, and that I would be safe with him if I decided to stay in the marriage. I could see that in a subtle way he was promoting my staying with Peter, but it was too late for that. I had made up my mind and I was resolute in my conviction to be free.

The Lama was wrong about Peter's being able to change. Peter has not changed his patterns to this day, and has in fact been divorced by a second wife, who could no longer tolerate his behavior and his treatment of her. Instead of leaving bankrupt as I had, she left with her health destroyed, dealing with the threat of impending stomach cancer. She received no help, no support from Peter or his family. His mother treated her exactly as she had treated me. Nothing had changed.

There was one young man in the practice group who reached out and supported me. He was eighteen years old and had helped his mom work with abused women. He saw all the classic signs of abuse that he had learned about while working with his mom, and he warned me of the possible tactics I could expect from Peter when I notified him of my decision. He was exactly right. When I told Peter I wanted a divorce, and that I had met with an attorney, he turned his abuse into affection. He wanted to have sex with me again.

My young friend had warned me that Peter would try to initiate having sex with me. He had read about it in a pamphlet from the women's shelter. It was a last-ditch effort to have power over me, to turn the tables, draw me back in and then dump me, giving him the upper hand. Armed with this insight, I was prepared. I rejected Peter and his advances, stood firm, resolute in my decision to divorce him and move forward with my life. I asked him to move out, with Luna standing at my side. It was over; the rest was paperwork and time.

My friend and his family were a great support to me in the days that followed, emotionally and financially. They invited me over to spend time at their home, where we enjoyed summer evenings on the porch. They were kind to my children and treated them like family. They also flew me in their private plane to an airport in Texas to pick up the car that Marie and her friends were giving me. Marie drove half way to meet us at the private airport.

I had to learn to stand on my own two feet, to maintain my direction, no matter how lost I found myself in life. I had to go deep within, find my strength, and assert my power over my life. I was not alone this time. I had support and encouragement from older, wiser women and their families. I had never previously allowed this form of support into my life.

I had met the Lama during my first week after moving to Taos, and had therefore credited my experiences, studies and practices that I'd learned from him with helping me gain the strength and confidence I needed to take back my life. My experience with the Lama ran parallel to my commitment to taking my life back. Yet it was not the source of my strength; it was not the underlying cause of my desire to take control of my life.

I realized I had decided to take control of my life when I witnessed and experienced the emotional trauma and devastation of the World Trade Center. I began taking steps to regain my freedom when I left Austin, Texas and moved back to Taos. I met the Lama, by chance, sitting in the waiting room of the Kundalini Center, whose program had inspired my move back to New Mexico. He was not the reason for the transformation in my life – *I* was. I was the creator of my awakening; the source of the light was within me. My guidance came from within my heart. I was following the light of my inner North Star.

I cleared my debts, divorced Peter and started a new life, all while living in Taos and studying the ancient practices. I falsely believed that my actions were the result of what I had learned from the Lama. I credited my accomplishments to the Lama, despite a lack of support from the group I practiced with and the Lama himself. When I reached out to the Lama, frightened and desperate for guidance, I found his door locked, my calls unanswered. I was forced to find my own path. Still, he was given credit for this as wisdom; wise counsel in the form of no counsel. Strange how willing I was to give him all the credit.

When I allow myself to go back to that time in my life, I realize that it was my own inner reflection that had empowered me. It was my willingness to listen to the voice within me, the wisdom of my heart that had propelled me forward. I became open to witnessing the signs that surrounded me, and willing to learn from them. I took my experiences and transformed them into strength. I became the creator of my life, and released the victim. I transformed suffering into light.

I shouldn't have given credit to the Lama for something I did entirely on my own, without support from him or anyone in the group we practiced with.

This was another example of how I continued to willingly give my power away, giving credit to others for the work that I myself had done. The truth is that the credit goes to me, and no one else. I stood up, made the decisions needed and took action. No one could do it for me. I did it. I recognized I was in trouble. I acknowledged my pattern, owned it and took responsibility for freeing myself. I sought help, took advice and followed through with my decisions. I took back my power. I recognized my pattern and released the part of myself that continued the cycle.

I have given up my power in so many ways in my life that I am continually looking for my pattern in all of my relationships and interactions. Peter's behavior was abusive and without integrity, and they supported him. That should have been enough for me to understand their true motivations, intentions and integrity. The actions of a person speak far more of their character than any words they might speak.

The Divorce Papers

The day I was to sign the divorce papers, I was at the park for Saturday practice with the Lama. I walked to my car to leave for the attorney's office; she had come in as a special courtesy for me to sign privately on the weekend. When I got to the car my hands wouldn't work. It was as if a force outside of myself was trying to prevent me from leaving. I couldn't get my hands to grasp; to bend and form around the handle of the car door. All my dexterity was gone, as if my fingers were frozen from the cold, swollen into blocks. Yet it was a warm summer day and my hands were fine only moments before.

There was nothing going to stop me, though. I didn't care how difficult it was, I was going to get to the attorney's office. It felt as though this force was purposely freezing me, holding me helpless, trying to prevent me from signing the divorce papers. I refused to give in to this energy. I used my wrists, in place of my hands, and forced the door open. Somehow I was able to maneuver the car and drive to the office using my wrists. I signed the divorce papers as I had intended, even though my hands were barely strong enough to form around the pen, swollen and cold, without blood flowing freely through them.

I decided I wouldn't take the abuse any longer. I wouldn't be a doormat who would rather will myself dead than stand up for myself. It was enough. I didn't keep Peter's name. I reclaimed Marcos' last name. I drove to Luna's house, exhausted and relieved to be free. It was done. I would have to wait six months, per New Mexico state law, for the judge to sign off and make it official, but I was officially free.

I acknowledge that there has been a pattern to my life. The root cause of the pattern has been my own lack of self-esteem and confidence. I can see it emerging in my relationships and interactions with others all the time. If I can maintain my self-esteem and confidence, I am free, my self-worth and identity secure. If I waver at all, surrender to the ideals, opinions or beliefs of someone other than myself, I am lost. If I lose focus for even a moment, stop making my own choices, I am back in the cycle. If I allow a spiritual teacher or guru the slightest advantage, believing they have access to wisdom that I do not, I am without power once again. If I surrender my will, my intentions, my desire to live the life I choose, I am lost.

I emerge from the cycle only when I recognize I am lost, awareness flooding my being. Only then can I stop and look within for direction. My own heart is my North Star, the light within guiding me, a beacon in the storm. I can always find my way by connecting to the true north within my heart, using the power of love to navigate my way back home, back to myself. Following the wisdom of my heart, I place my hand to my chest, breathe through my heart and remember with every cell of my being the joys I have known in my life, then I ask silently within, "What do you want me to know? What do you want me to do? What is the most effective solution?"

I forgive myself for giving away my power, for believing and accepting false concepts of who I am, for trusting others to know better than I know for myself. I am worthy of receiving, with gratitude, the credit for my efforts and my victories. I am responsible for my choices in life, and I am deserving of accolades when I get it right. I am powerful and not afraid to own my power, to step fully into who I am.

Moved to Santa Fe

I read an ad in the newspaper that offered an apartment I could afford in the neighborhood I was looking for. I drove to Santa Fe one evening to preview the apartment, as the landlord said it was open and available to see anytime. I knew right away that it was perfect. It was immaculate, with a small kiva fireplace, spacious kitchen and updated appliances. There was a private, fenced backyard for the kids and a nice front patio, shaded with trees, for hanging out. I called and secured the apartment immediately. My young friend from the group and his family helped me by paying the deposit up front until I had the funds to pay them back. They even let me borrow their Suburban to make multiple trips, bringing all of my belongings to my new apartment.

I slept on a futon in the living room of the 650-square-foot apartment, and gave the kids the bedroom with bunk beds. The bedroom was filled with light from the sliding glass doors leading to the backyard. I was given several pieces of furniture from my friend's family that fit the small size of my apartment perfectly. I hung my own artwork on the walls, and created a beautiful space for my kids and me to begin our healing journey.

I moved to Santa Fe, New Mexico, with Felipe and Indigo, as a single mom with two children to protect. The Lama had moved to Santa Fe, and a few of his devoted students followed, myself included. I had still not recognized my pattern in this relationship, and I followed him blindly. Indigo was two years old and Felipe was eight. I enrolled Felipe in first grade in a new school, and we began a new life.

The kids and I were happy; we had all the freedom we wanted. I was on food stamps to make ends meet; we never wanted for anything and always had plenty. I tried to work, but because of Felipe's Social Security benefits, we only qualified for four hours a week of childcare from the Children Youth and Families Department (CYFD). I did my best. I found a job as an assistant to a writer and helped organize her life, thanks to my friend Marie.

I loved my time with Luna. She had been a saving grace to me more than once, opening her heart and her home to me without hesitation or question. But it was time for me to step out on my own if I was going to stop repeating patterns. She was sad to see us leave, and supported me fully, knowing I had to grow and move forward in my life. It was time for me to use my own voice, my own power and make my own decisions for what was best for my children and me. I had to become self-reliant, responsible and independent. The only way to do that was to live on my own; it was a necessary next step.

The only problem was that I was still giving my power away. I was following – not a husband, this time, but a guru – from place to place. I still couldn't step outside of myself and gain clarity on this relationship. I couldn't understand that I had removed myself from a co-dependent marriage, only to replace it with a co-dependent guru-disciple relationship. I had made the transfer of dependency simultaneously, a seamless transition without awareness. The Lama had made it clear with a ritual ceremony, where the student asked three times of the Lama to become a disciple – and with his final consent, it would be granted. Those twelve students had committed to follow his practices to the end, and they would begin teaching others when the time was right. I was one of the twelve, the only woman.

My divorce became final a few months after I moved to Santa Fe. I was officially and legally free from my second marriage. I had replaced this relationship with a fully committed relationship to a guru, with complete adherence to his practices, in a ritualistic field of study. There was not a beat skipped, a single breath inhaled, where I truly stood free in the strength and wisdom of my own being. It took me years to acknowledge this choice and to admit that it was true. I denied it, renounced all responsibility for this decision, for over twelve years.

Chapter 17
I Met Jack

The man responsible for making my new apartment so nice, so immaculately cleaned, repaired and updated, was the property manager for the apartments. His name was simple – Jack. He was tall, six foot nine inches, with dirty-blonde hair and bright-blue eyes. He was kind and gentle considering his height, strength and years in the trades. He was very funny, and extremely protective of the tenants. He treated them as if they were family. He was always watching, making sure everyone was okay, especially the single moms and seniors.

He was a caring soul who helped the tenants as best he could. He would let them know if they were behind on their rent, telling them that they had better get caught up because the landlord was going to evict them any day. He would run interference on their behalf, telling the landlord that he would lose money repairing the apartment as the tenant had been there for many years and there would be lots of updating to do. The cost of repairs and time lost due to renovation would more than surpass the overdue amount. He was a voice for those without a voice. All he wanted was for things to be fair.

His sole intent was to protect and care for people, although he was always shy, about admitting it. He provided a compassionate ear, and would get the tenant's needs in front of the owner so that they would be addressed. He had a kind heart and a boisterous temperament, always willing to laugh and have fun. He was also extremely sensitive, which was a gift and a curse. It made him care about the needs of others; it also made him quick to react, to defend what he believed to be true and right. He was always clear and definitive about where he stood on issues. If he felt something was not fair or just, he would speak up, and define the appropriate boundary with confidence and strength.

When I first saw Jack, he scared me. He made eye contact with me from across the street in the far parking lot, as I was moving in to my new apartment. Next thing I knew, he was knocking on my door, identifying himself as the property manager. He was so tall, his presence commanding, his sky-blue eyes intent, as he focused on me while searching the room behind me. I could hear that his voice was gentle and non-threatening, but it didn't help. It didn't change my being frightened of this giant man standing at my door. I was a single mom in a new neighborhood. I felt vulnerable, a target to be taken advantage of.

If he was the property manager, how would I hide my kids from his prying eyes? I had never let the landlord know that I had two kids. I didn't think he would rent a one-bedroom apartment to me if he knew. That was all I could afford, and it was perfect for us, just across the street from Felipe's new school. I was terrified that this man was not who he was claiming to be. I was also terrified that it *was* true, and that he would let the landlord know – or that he would tell me I couldn't live in a one-bedroom apartment with my two kids.

Jack could see I was uncomfortable. I was thankful he didn't force his way in or press me for information. Instead he backed up, gave me space, respected my boundary and told me that the landlord had not let him know that he had rented the apartment. He explained that this was why he had come, to check out what was going on. He needed to replace one more section of the blinds on the sliding-glass door in the back of the apartment before he felt it was ready to be leased. He was the one who had done all of the repairs; he'd painted it, cleaned it and made it ready.

The whole time he stood at the door I kept it cracked, almost closed, with me inside. He slowly bent down and placed the slat for the long vertical blind on the porch, to the far side of my door, and backed away. He told me how it to install it by clicking it into place on the top clip, and left me to take care of it myself. I waited until I could see he had gone before I reached out and grabbed the blind, quickly pulling it back into the apartment.

Jack was always at the apartments, as he had two more, on either side of my apartment, to remodel and prepare for rental. It took him two days to realize I had kids. He liked kids, and he immediately waved and said hi to them. It didn't matter at all to him that I was a single mom with two kids in a one-bedroom apartment. Instead of telling the landlord or giving me a hard time, he looked out for us.

One day there was a woman who had gotten lost and was wandering around the apartments. She had been drinking, and had staggered close to my front door. I was unaware, but Jack was watching. He went over to the woman and asked if he could give her a ride somewhere, which he did. When he got back, he knocked on my door and let me know that he had taken the woman somewhere safe. I didn't even know she was there; he was afraid the kids would see her in that condition and wanted to protect them from experiencing that. Not only had he protected me and my family, he had helped get that poor woman to safety. That was just how Jack was.

Indigo Sick

As the months passed and the weather vacillated between winter and spring, Indigo became sick, throwing up and running a fever. I took her to the emergency room, where Felipe, Indigo and I waited for hours, with no food. It was midnight before we were able to see the doctor. His solution to our fear? A popsicle, to remedy her vomiting and fever. We had waited hours for her to receive a popsicle. I was dumbfounded. I was dismayed that we had waited so long, with no dinner, just so Indigo could be given a popsicle.

I saw Jack working on the apartments the day after my emergency-room visit and told him my story of the night before. I could tell him anything and he would listen, take it to heart and give me his honest opinion. I relayed to him the highlights, the long wait in the emergency room with no dinner, only for Indigo to receive a popsicle for her vomiting and fever. He said, without flinching, "Why didn't you call me? I would've gotten Happy Meals for the kids." I would never have thought of calling him. To him, it was common sense to provide help to a single mom in need. It was also a given that he considered me a friend, and that I could call on him if I needed help.

This was not the same reaction from my so called spiritual friends and co-disciples of the Lama. None of them offered any help. I had told them that Indigo was sick, and that I was afraid I needed to take her to the emergency room. I even called to tell them when I was about to drive to the emergency room. These were my spiritual friends; we had all moved to Santa Fe at the same time, and we were supposed to be close. We had created a close-knit family during our mediation practices, or so I had thought. They knew I was struggling and offered no tangible help – no commonsense action to be of service or lend a helping hand.

Peter was living in town; he had moved to Santa Fe at the same time I had, along with the other devoted students. He didn't come, either. His boss said he could leave work early, but he didn't. Here was Jack, the property manager, saying, "I would have brought you food. Why didn't you call me? I would have helped," when no one else was willing to be there.

Like all the tenants, I had become friends with Jack. He was always willing to chat while he worked. I would visit him often, asking for help with simple things like prying the bit out of my new drill, or helping me get the right-sized bolts to put the bunk beds together. He was continually repairing, cleaning and remodeling the apartments after a tenant moved out, or making them better for those who lived there. Jack was always available to lend a helping hand, and he never complained that I or anyone else was taking him away from the work he had to get done.

Jack had opinions about everything, and he was surprisingly well versed in many areas of life. He loved to share stories and could talk with ease to anyone, no matter what background they came from. He didn't care if they were rich or poor; a man, woman, child – everyone was the same to him. He was respectful and honest, and he had a sense of humor, no matter what.

Jack had a commonsense approach to life, which always surprised me and caught me off guard. I used so little common sense to make my decisions. I approached life through feelings, following an unseen guidance, using my emotions and intuition to make decisions. He used facts, asked questions and garnered information from experts. He would then run his thoughts by trusted friends before finally making a decision. He was exceedingly responsible with money, saving more than half of his income with every paycheck. He had goals and pursued them relentlessly.

Chapter 18

Began Dating

I began dating Jack a few months after Indigo's illness and recovery. I had begun hanging out with him more and more as he worked – getting to know his values – while Felipe was at school and Indigo napped. We went on dates when the kids went to stay the weekend with Peter. Peter would take Felipe, along with Indigo, as it was easier for him to have them both. Felipe helped look after Indigo and kept her company while Peter worked on the computer. Felipe knew only Peter as his father, as his own had died when he was a newborn. It made sense to have him go with Indigo for her custody visits. Indigo didn't like to go to Peter's without him, and he was able to tell me if anything inappropriate happened while they were with Peter.

I became nervous committing to another relationship, new to my divorce, with weekly custody visits to remind me of what I had escaped. I began doubting my ability not to repeat my pattern. When I met Jack, I was still blaming Marcos for being strong when I was weak, for having confidence when mine was lacking. I still sought clothes that would hide my insecurities. I blamed Peter for spending all of my money and being abusive. I was in denial that I had given my power to the Lama in hopes of being seen as special – good enough to receive enlightenment. I was still not in a place of ownership, of taking responsibility for my choices and my pattern of co-dependence. I was still actively playing the role of victim in life.

My experience with Peter had me on the defensive, distrusting. He lived a few blocks away and was still causing me to struggle, not paying child support on time, not complying with the rules of the divorce. He still wanted to be in control and have me beaten down; it made him feel more confident if I was weak. He felt threatened by my presence at the Lama's classes and would find ways to fight with me during the sessions or make me feel uncomfortable. After class, he and the other guys would follow the Lama to his apartment for their private, men-only sessions. I tried to follow, and was told I was not permitted to attend.

I continued to be devoted to the Lama, attending classes every Saturday, giving away my power without hesitation. I listened to him as if he were a god. Every word he said held meaning and significance. He was a guru who was wise enough to say he was not a guru. He insisted he was a friend, a co-traveler on our shared journey through life, seeking enlightenment. He just happened to have more gifts, knowledge and understanding than we did.

I was timid, frightened of being on my own, living in an apartment alone with the kids. I compensated by acting as if I were invincible. I would walk like a soldier, shoulders back, eyes forward, chin held high. Everything about me said "Keep back; I'm damaged," when I began dating Jack. I would get close to Jack physically, not trust myself and prickle at his affection. I had so many conflicting feelings within me – and I was receiving so much guidance from outside of myself that I didn't know who to trust. Everyone thought they knew what was best for me. They were fearful that I would get hurt again, that I couldn't make it on my own. No one asked me what I thought. I had proven myself incapable of taking care of myself and my children. I was in a constant battle to have my voice be heard, and to make my own choices.

I didn't know what I wanted from one moment to the next. All I knew was that I felt safe with Jack. He was honest and direct, and he had integrity. All he ever wanted was to protect me and to make me happy. He challenged me with commonsense questions, and didn't tolerate bullshit of any kind. He could see through my every explanation – or excuse, as he called them. He cared about my kids and looked out for them. He reminded me of my need to be grounded, and he put my children and responsibilities first – despite my beliefs and feelings regarding my spiritual practices.

I pushed my childhood friend, Marie, away at this time. I simply had too many voices, too many witnesses offering guidance and direction. I left a message on her voicemail one day, saying, "I love you, but I can no longer be your friend. I wish you all the best in getting your acupuncture license and I hope you have a wonderful future. Please do not call me again." She didn't call. I lost her as my witness and friend for over a decade.

I pushed her away because she expressed alarm and concern regarding my meeting Jack so quickly after my divorce, and hearing about my practices and devotion to the Lama. I couldn't hear or accept what she had to say at the time. I wasn't ready to acknowledge and address my patterns. Jack and I would get into big fights after I talked to her on the phone. He could sense that Marie wasn't speaking well of him, and he didn't appreciate her interference. The conflict was uncomfortable for me, so I took what I realize now was the cowardly way out.

I missed Marie's wedding and the birth of her twin sons, which I will always regret. We have since reconnected and begun a new relationship, although I feel I will never be as close to Marie as I had once been. I hurt her so deeply when I left that voicemail message. She has since forgiven me for shutting her out, and I know we care for one another deeply, without question. I listen to the wisdom she has to offer, and I honor and respect her friendship. Jack understands that she is not a threat and enjoys my having a girlfriend to share with, one who has known me through it all.

Moved In

I moved in with Jack four months after we began dating, in a time of chaos, in the midst of a storm raging, with me holding on by a thread. He said it would be cheaper, and that I really couldn't afford to live in the apartments and take care of the kids on what I was earning. I only had four hours a week with childcare to work, as Indigo wasn't in school yet. That would never be enough time to make the money I needed. If I had never married Peter, I would still have my Social Security benefits as Marcos' widow, as well as Felipe's, but that was not the case. I did my best, given the finite tools and resources I had at the time. Jack insisted I get a job and become independent. I had kids who relied on me, and it was time I stood up and took care of business. He would pay for the house and all the bills; all I needed to do was pay for food and for my kids' expenses.

Jack thought I'd be a good fit for selling real estate. His last two girlfriends had worked as receptionists for real estate companies. He had encouraged them to get licensed, but they didn't feel they could pass the licensing exam. I was smart, the top of my class in high school and college. That wouldn't be a problem for me. He felt it was a good career and a way to make good money quickly, which I needed to do.

I made the argument to him that I had no sense of direction; that my sister used to tell me, "You couldn't find your way out of a paper bag." I wasn't social by any means; I was uncomfortable and insecure around people. I didn't do social networking or have any friends that I could market a home to. The only friends that I still had were people from the spiritual practices. They couldn't be bothered to help me when my child was sick, and they certainly weren't going to buy a home through me.

That didn't matter to Jack. "You need to get some self-confidence. You could make a lot of money in real estate. You're smart, but if you want to work all your life for minimum wage that's your choice. I'm going to retire and start remodeling and building my own properties and retire to an island. I'm going to go fishing and have fun, but you can stay here and work for the rest of your life."

I ordered the real-estate sales course online, and began studying to take the real-estate exams at both the state and national levels. The school offered in-person classes in my area, but I wasn't comfortable attending class to study for the course. After a few months with the online course, entirely on my own, I had studied and passed both exams – and I became licensed to sell real estate in New Mexico in 2004.

I had the old car that Marie had given me, which now needed a new muffler. I sounded like a gangster driving down the street. When the car idled, it was so loud that it sounded out of control. How was I supposed to take someone out to look for properties when it was evident that I couldn't even afford an apartment? I was embarrassed and confused, my self-esteem plummeting even more.

I contacted the manager for the new-agent division at an international real-estate firm, and requested an interview to qualify to hang my license with them. Jack had said that this company was the one that I should interview with, and request to work with as an independent contractor. They were the best company in town, and their brokers made the highest incomes.

I parked my car far away from the office and walked in for my interview. I was given the opportunity on the spot. I was very excited about this, and I was excited to begin a new career and a new life with Jack. I knew I would need new clothes and a better car to pull this off. They had asked me in the interview if I had a reliable, quality car. I said yes. I wasn't lying; it was a Toyota – just not a new one.

Married Third Time

I told Jack that I had no intention of being a forty-year-old girlfriend. I wanted and needed stability; I had kids to consider. He had been in a long-term relationship, lasting fifteen years, and had never married. He was eight years my senior, responsible to a fault and a diehard romantic. I knew he understood my concerns, but he had many deep-seated fears about relationships after being taken advantage of before, and being used for his generosity and kindheartedness.

I asked him one night, after watching a particularly romantic and sentimental movie about a divorcee finding love again, if he would marry me. He said yes. It was that simple and without fanfare. We knew what kind of life and family we wanted to create together. Now that I had a job in place, Jack was willing to marry me. He was not going to have someone live off him. I had to carry my own weight, my equal share.

We got married on my birthday, in September, 2004, at City Hall, for $35. My sister Katelyn and my mom came. Jack's mom and best friend also came, as well as our accountant and his wife. A friend of Jack's and his wife left flowers on our doorstep. I carried those flowers with me to City Hall. There was no fuss. My sister teased me, taking a picture of a parolee behind me as he was arriving to check in for his court date.

When we entered the courtroom for the ceremony, the heavy metal door closed loudly behind us. Jack was panic stricken – as the sound of that door closing seemed to hit home, cementing his acceptance to take responsibility for a wife and her two young children. He was thirty-nine years old at the time. He had hoped to be retired soon, working on his own properties. That dream was fading fast as he took on responsibility for a young family.

When we said our vows, I thought he was going to pass out. The judge checked to see if he was all right before proceeding with the vows. Jack persevered, remaining upright for the entire ceremony – and he has been steadfast, at my side, ever since. It was official; I had been married for the third time at just past thirty years old. I had been recognized legally by six different names – widowed, divorced and now married again.

The week after our wedding, Jack searched the car magazines and local ads and found me a Dodge Stratus, in like-new condition, that I could use for my real-estate practice. We bought it on a rare cloudy day in New Mexico. When I woke up the next morning and looked out the window, I realized I had a purple car, the color of Barney. I couldn't believe it. The car looked navy blue without the light of the sun. Jack wanted me to know he was willing to invest some money into my success, and that he believed I could do it. Now I was committed to making it in real estate.

Chapter 19

Began Fighting

Our first fight had been over my devotion to the Lama and my practices. I took Jack to meet the Lama, and he fell asleep on the floor while the Lama was talking. I was so mad at him, and I felt so embarrassed. On the drive home, he said, "That guy is an egotistical asshole, and if you are so in love with him you should go marry *him*. All he did was talk about himself. He didn't ask me a single question or engage anyone else in the conversation. All he did was talk, while you sat there paying attention only to him."

I was hurt and confused. My relationship was purely platonic with the Lama. I couldn't understand why Jack felt so threatened, why his need to protect me had been triggered so strongly. I defended the Lama, and my practices, vehemently. I was a devoted disciple, and if Jack couldn't accept that, I would leave. I believed that the Lama was a gifted and wise spiritual teacher, and I would not be deterred from my practices.

Jack gave in. He didn't want to lose me. He watched and continued to protect me, quietly, without my knowing. He was always listening – watching and fighting with me when need be – if I went too far adrift. I couldn't understand his intentions. I attacked him without mercy if he said or did anything that I felt threatened my devotion to the Lama.

We began fighting in earnest during the two weeks before our wedding – and we continued for the next twelve years. I threatened repeatedly to divorce him. He told me to move out on an almost-weekly basis, though we never parted. We couldn't stand to be separated from one another for any length of time. Our love has always been intense, passionate and fierce in every way. Eventually we will learn to give up the fighting altogether, as we always end up in the same place anyway. We love each other, for better or worse, and that's all right.

At six foot nine inches tall, Jack can be intimidating. In arguments he can unleash a fury of curse words, spitting venom across the room, as only someone with a lifetime in the trades can do. He has always been expressive and passionate, hands flying, jumping up and down. In an argument, it can feel overwhelming to be close to him. He puts out so much emotion; bursts of intensity emanate from his being, forcefully exploding into my being. I have learned to let it pass through me, over me and around me, leaving me untouched. I smile, or look away, until it passes. Once he has spun it all out of his system and has come to his final conclusion, he expresses what he always does – that he is sorry he was upset, and that he knows it does no good. He has arrived at acceptance. He cares – that's what makes him passionate. And he hates injustice with an intensity that few can comprehend. I get it, and we move on.

He was afraid of being taken advantage of, losing all that he had worked so hard for. I was reckless with money, giving it away to gurus and spiritual teachers, attending seminars and lectures. I had to assure him repeatedly that I had no intention of taking his money, using him or taking advantage of his deep love for me. He was afraid of my truly knowing how much he loved me, and at the same time he demanded my acknowledgment of his deep love. He wanted me to understand, and be compassionate, while at the same time he pretended to be aloof.

He became my sharpening stone. When I felt beaten down by life, I would fight back with him. I gave him no slack. I interpreted his every suggestion as an effort to control me. I would neither tolerate nor allow him to control me in any way. Instead, I gave my power away to every other person in my life. Jack alone was the person I would stand up to, be strong and fight for my voice. I would not be silenced. He took the brunt of all of my suffering. I attacked *him* for every person I allowed to control, abuse and silence me.

Jack was the only one telling me the truth, the commonsense truth, as he saw it. He never bought into any of my spiritual practices. He watched from the outside, seeing the parlor tricks for what they were, ploys of the ego. He had a way of summing up the intentions of a person within minutes of meeting them. His years of working as a bouncer in Los Angeles night clubs had honed his skills to perfection. He has always called people on their "bullshit," as he puts it. He has no fear of the repercussions of speaking his truth. He's willing to suffer the consequences, rather than be silenced. If he finds that his truth has caused someone harm, he softens the blow – apologizing or tempering the effect – but he never backs down.

Through the process of fighting in this way, we learned to trust each other unconditionally. There was no doubt that we loved each other dearly and would do anything for each other. I was terrified of getting lost, my pattern re-emerging. I resisted his every suggestion, his every effort to protect me. All he ever wanted was for me to be happy, to be successful and independent. He respected me and wanted me to respect myself. Jack would tell me he never had any intention of controlling me. He wanted an equal partner – and he would accept nothing less. He fought to make me stand up to everyone else in my life. He demanded that I become an equal in every way, whether I believed I was ready or not. I fought back, resisting his every effort to help propel me forward. I was in survival mode, and I saw him as the enemy.

I never backed down in my fights with Jack; my voice, my choice were going to be heard. For some reason, with him alone, it mattered. It mattered to me that he acknowledged my truth, right or wrong. I learned to stand, calm and steadfast, in the eye of the storm. I learned to hold on until the raging winds passed, knowing that peace and love would return without question. Never again would I allow another husband to take my power. Eventually I would take my experiences, the skills I had learned in my conflicts with Jack, and apply them to all areas of my life.

The Pattern Repeats

I began working as an independent contractor in real estate in October, shortly after our wedding. I took training classes, created a website, mailed out introductory letters to my neighborhood and went on tours to learn the different areas of the market and the inventory available. Each month I had desk fees, advertising and other expenses. Jack was paying for it all. He was frustrated, and becoming resentful, by December. I wasn't doing enough; I had to get out there and go after it if I was going to be successful. I needed to study the market the way he did, for hours each day, and really get into it and push.

I had no interest in researching properties on the internet. I had no interest in sales. I wasn't a salesperson by any stretch of the imagination. Frustrated and unwilling to put up any more money, he told me to quit, saying real estate wasn't for me. I submitted a letter to my manager to terminate my contract, and I thought I was done. But my manager liked me, and before I left real estate, he asked if I would be willing to see if I could become an assistant to one of the top brokers. I interviewed and got a job with a top broker at the company. Jack was elated – I would be successful, and I would have an income while I learned the business.

In the beginning, I learned a lot, and I also had fun. I worked long hours, weekends, snow days and through my kids' special events. Sometimes I worked two weeks straight in the office, and on call, before I had any break at all. I would still have to take calls, if they came in, even on my precious days off. I had to multitask, make arrangements and coordinate, even while I was driving from one property to the next. I was showing property and trying to manage the paperwork for contracts, even when I was out of the office. I had to create the documents; scan, file and get signatures from all parties. I had to respond to all emails and phone calls immediately. I had to be available for all the other brokers – who preferred to call and coordinate with me, rather than with my boss, who had a reputation for not being accommodating or agreeable. That was my job, to make it all happen – that's what I was paid for.

I had to carry keys to every home, and remember alarm codes for all the properties. Sometimes there were more than thirty listings. I needed to be ready in case someone decided they wanted to see a property without warning. I was never to say no and not show a property, unless I was unable to get the seller's approval. I could never say no because I couldn't personally make it happen.

I would speed, racing to get to yet another property at a moment's notice. I was showing high-end, luxury properties, with outrageous square footages. I had to make each home show-ready in minutes. Most of the properties were second homes that were closed up while the owner was away. The security measures alone were enough to make me crazy.

Every house had its own set of rules. I was running through the homes, turning off lights and closing blinds – each one as the seller had specified – and double-checking all the doors. Some homeowners would only accept the blinds with the slats pointing down, or raised or lowered to the exact angle they preferred. I had to remember every nuance of every home and homeowner, while running as fast as I could.

I had to cover it all and get to the next property, never appearing unprepared, exhausted, disheveled or out of sorts. I had to smile, put on a happy face, and be a gracious and good girl, professional at all times. My tattoos had to be covered, even in the hottest weather. I was wearing long sleeves to hide who I was, fearful of not being accepted or judged at a glance.

I did it all with the support of the real-estate staff at the company office. They were my saving grace. They were kind, compassionate and supportive. They knew the pressure I was under and did all they could to help me in any way, even listening to me complain and vent when I couldn't hold it in any longer. Other brokers in the office, and those who understood the pressure I was under, were supportive and encouraging. The crazy thing was that I cared deeply for my boss. I was protective of her in every way and treated her like family. In short, I loved her – and she chose to use my love to her advantage.

When a multi-million-dollar property sold, I would receive a minuscule $200, which eventually increased to $250 per sale. I would receive a bi-weekly salary and a year-end bonus, which made things a little better. In my best year I made close to $60,000, while the broker I gave everything for netted a six-figure income. She did the negotiating and attended the closings. I did everything else. She would cover when and where she decided, mostly for appearances at showings where she thought someone important was going to be in attendance. If the property, client or other broker was difficult, it was mine to handle. If she expressed any discomfort about something, I would do my best to make it better.

Her husband was not well, causing her to leave town for weeks at a time. At one point, her husband was at the Mayo clinic for tests for nearly two months. I covered everything by myself – all the showings, contracts and clients. Still, to her, I was nothing more than an assistant. She even told me she would never make me an equal partner. I should have stopped, left, and found another job – or gone out on my own in real estate. Instead, I made excuses for her behavior. She was incapable of ever seeing me as anything more than a commodity to be used.

Other brokers would ask me how I dealt with her. I always told them that she was really very compassionate; she just had a rigid and tough exterior. I'm not certain that she could ever trust anyone enough to lower her wall of protection. I was the closest person to her – I forgave her all her indecencies – and I only ever gave her love in return. I never pointed out her mistakes; I would just cover them, smooth them over and move on.

Other brokers would see me running – literally running down the halls, desperately trying to make it to the next appointment. Every summer I would become rail thin, never having time to stop, eat lunch, have a snack or nurture my body. The other brokers in the company would volunteer to help, without compensation of any kind, knowing I was drowning in responsibility. I had to turn down their kind offers. My boss would never allow it, especially while she was away. She was too afraid someone would try to steal her client away or take a portion of her commission. I was on my own, for better or worse.

She went on trips and vacations whenever she decided. I had to ask, and get her permission, before I could plan anything. I could never do anything of my own on weekends or holidays, which she thought were important to her family, or at times when she had planned to take a trip herself. Her step-kids were grown adults with their own families. I had two small children at home – but this didn't matter to her. My life was completely out of balance. I was never around for my kids. They were carted off to after-school and summer programs. I was exhausted when I was home, and fighting with Jack on a regular basis. I was unhappy and stressed out – but the bills were being paid.

Jack was experiencing an almost identical situation at his job as a property manager. The stress was overwhelming for both of us. There were no boundaries for either of us. Work ruled our lives, as we ran our bodies into the ground for our bosses. We had the same desire to please others and be of genuine service. We disregarded our own needs for the needs of our bosses. We cared for them like family, devoted to making life better for them, while neglecting our own family. We believed in the end that we would be rewarded for our dedication – but it never happened.

Despite my efforts, my pattern continued. I was fighting for my life on more than one front. I was being controlled and manipulated at work, instead of being controlled and manipulated at home by my husband. I couldn't break free of this cycle, this pattern of giving away my power. I was still oblivious to my pattern – and how, at this time, it was being expressed through spiritual teachers and gurus. I was now facing, and beginning to understand, the complexity of the power exchange between an employer and an employee in a work relationship.

The only respite I had to these lessons came through awareness. If I could just gain awareness of the cycle, of my surrendering my power, for one moment, I could break free. The only way I gained awareness was through direct experience – that was the only way I could regain my power and stand up. I had to understand the psychology and philosophy of it all, in physical form. Merely speaking about philosophies and theories alone meant nothing. I had to feel them in my physical body as true and real. The difficulty was that once I learned to recognize and feel the pattern in one relationship, it expressed itself in another. It was as if I could never fully break free. I was continually being drained of my power, strength and confidence. I was being forced to learn my pattern, in its every aspect, in all possible scenarios. I had to learn to be in a relationship, and not be consumed by it – to be the drop of water and the whole ocean at once.

The root cause remained the same, a lack of self-esteem and confidence. If I could focus on maintaining my self-esteem, I would create healthy boundaries and relationships. Those boundaries would give me the confidence I needed to stand up and be my own advocate. Boundaries allowed me to show myself and others that I deserved to be valued and respected. I was worthy of promotion, good pay, success, acceptance, love and friendship. My relationships reflected my inner beliefs. There was no hiding the truth behind affirmations, declarations, meditations or practices.

Hernia

One day at work I saw an email offering an agent's personal items for sale. One of the items was a large Trinitron TV – one of the old TVs that had a large screen and a giant back end to match. They were enormous. We only had the small TV that Jack had when we got married, so I asked if he wanted to go see if this TV might be a good deal.

When I called the broker, she said, "Bring a few guys with you – this thing is huge." Jack of course said, "No, we can do it if we want it." We bought it, and he and the broker's husband carried it to the truck.

When we got home, I told Jack that he'd better call one of his friends to help unload it. He said no. He hated to ask anyone for help – *I* was his help. I tried to lift it. I could barely raise it an inch from the back of the truck. I asked again for him to call for help.

Now he was pissed. He told me, "If you want the fucking thing, *you* bring it in. Otherwise I'm leaving it here." He headed back to the house. I retaliated, "If you wanted a man for a partner, why didn't you just marry one?" He was adamant that we had to be equals; we had to do everything on our own. The only problem was that I wasn't a six foot nine man. I was five foot eight inches and barely 120 pounds. I had not spent a lifetime in the trades, building the muscles and the wisdom to lift objects greater than my own weight. I was a woman; how was I supposed to be his equal physically too?

Storm clouds were overhead; it would rain by evening. I knew I had to get the TV into the house or it would be destroyed. I knew he was pissed off, and there would be no way to talk him into calling for help. I would have to find a way. I stopped and studied the situation. The truck was backed in by the wood pile. There was a small hill, a way to get around most of the steps to the front door. I could do it. I would have to focus with my entire mind, but I knew I could do it. I would have to command my body to override its warnings. I had learned in childhood that I could make my mind shut off the pain and force my body to go beyond its limits. That was how I was able to deliver Felipe, when I ripped my insides apart.

I called Jack back outside and told him I could make it work. Once I was able to lift it past the back end of the truck, and take a few steps, I knew it was only a matter of focus and determination. I lifted the TV with Jack and carried it to the house. Every few steps it would slice deeply into my soft hands, cutting into my flesh. I would have to stop, put it down, breathe, focus and begin again. I was determined, inspired by each step closer I came to the house. I continued, up the four steps that could not be avoided, and into the house. I rested and carried it one more time to its final destination. Jack was amazed, impressed. He couldn't believe I had done it. He was proud of me. I was shocked. He was proud of the sheer stupidity of my decision.

He knew all along that it was too great a burden for me. I was dumbfounded that he was impressed that I was willing to put myself in danger because he threatened to leave the TV in the rain. He had tricked me into doing what I believed I couldn't do, and he was impressed when I found a way to overcome the obstacle. Jack saw this as my being willing to do more than I thought possible; a good thing. I saw it as manipulation and pure stupidity.

The next day, my body was so sore I could barely move. Every muscle had been tested beyond its limits. I took off my clothes and stepped into the shower to wash away the memory of the pain from my body. I let the sun come in from the window and bathe me in light. I looked down and noticed a bulge in my pelvic region. I pressed, and felt it squish beneath my fingers. There was a hole I could push my fingers into below the squishy flesh. I had not noticed this before. I had no idea what it was.

I got out of the shower, dried off and showed it to Jack. He knew immediately, "You have a hernia. Shit, you must have gotten it from carrying the TV. What the fuck? You might need to have surgery to fix that. That could cost thousands." I didn't want to believe it, but he was right. It was true. I looked up hernias on the internet and conceded.

I pressed the flesh back into the hole, as if it had never happened, but the second I breathed or lifted anything, the bulge would pop out again. I asked around and found a surgeon that people recommended in town, and called him directly for an appointment. We had only catastrophic insurance, so this would be mostly an out-of-pocket expense.

The doctor examined me and discovered that I actually had two forms of hernia. One they called the typical women's, the other the typical man's. The first was high at the top of my stomach, probably from my pushing Felipe out during labor when I thought he was in danger, ripping my insides to shreds. The second was low in my pelvic region from picking up the TV, the typical man's hernia from the exertion of lifting.

The doctor told Jack, "Next time, call some guys to help. Don't ask your wife to move anything like that again. She's way too small to carry that kind of thing." Jack was embarrassed and ashamed by the directness of the doctor. He never liked anyone to say that he wasn't considerate and helpful to others. He wanted to protect me, not hurt me. He had let his need to be independent, to not bother anyone else and ask for help, to override his common sense and allow me to be hurt. I was the only one he ever treated this way, demanding I could do more than I thought possible. He expected me to be his equal in all ways. He would point out that other guys weren't as strong as he was all the time. He always believed I was powerful, stronger than I believed I was. He would accept nothing less from me than my best.

In the operating room I was charged double, for two surgeries, as I had two hernia operations performed. The total cost was over $10,000. Jack would joke that it was the most expensive TV we ever bought. I was stitched together and had a permanent patch placed in my pelvis to hold my guts inside. The doctor had taken longer than expected, as my other hernia was like "Swiss cheese," in his words, with shredded intestines to be mended.

When they tried to get me to wake up after the surgery, they couldn't. I kept passing out. They gave me fructose syrup to jolt me into consciousness. They had to get me to the bathroom to pee before I could leave. I passed out again in the bathroom. Their solution was to put me in a wheelchair and roll me out the back door. But Jack was nowhere to be found.

He hated hospitals and doctors after his dad's long battle and death from leukemia. He was so worried about me, and my having surgery, that he took off and left while it was happening. He took himself and the kids to McDonalds for breakfast. I was constantly misinterpreting his heart and intentions, and I saw it as abandonment, as his not caring. I couldn't see it as a sign of his profound love for me.

The nurses were able to reach him by phone, and they directed him to pull around to the back door to pick me up. When he pulled up, I was giving him the stink eye and he knew it. I was always mad at him, which only made matters worse. He never wanted to disappointment me or let me down, ever. He wanted to make me happy, to be my hero. The harder he tried, the worse he made it.

I continued to pass out repeatedly when we got home. Any exertion would cause me to pass out, and the pain was so intense, I would wake in a pool of sweat. My body was trying to cope with the stress, and failing. Jack would have to half-carry me to use the bathroom. I had a pain ball that fed a continual dose of pain medicine into my body, but it wasn't working.

Two days later, my mom flew in from New York to help me recover. She helped me get up and move around a little more each day. The pain ball emptied, and I removed it. I was popping pain pills like crazy. Jack freaked out and told me to stop. He was terrified I was becoming an addict at record speed.

I talked with my grandma, who told me to stop taking them altogether. She shared that she'd had reactions to pain meds, and thought I might be having the same problem. I listened to her and stopped cold turkey. With each passing hour I felt better, and four hours after I stopped all pain medication I was fine. I was up, and walking about, with bearable pain. It was a reaction to the pain medicine that had created the unbearable pain – causing me to pass out so that I was barely able to stand erect. My recovery was steady after that.

I had missed a week of work, and my boss was anxious to have me get back. My mom left and I resumed, as best I could for as long as I could each day, until I was back at record speed. I never stopped to consider how selfish and inconsiderate this expectation was. I was a commodity to be used; there was nothing left for me. It was as if my boss wanted to keep me running, and never let me stand still, so I could take a moment to gain awareness and say, "No. Hell no. I'm not doing this anymore."

Chapter 20

Pregnant Viktor

I had two abortions out of my fear of repeating old patterns, and because of Jack's fear of the cost of being a parent. Pregnant for the third time, I refused to have another abortion. The Lama still influenced my life, although we now had limited contact. He had told me I would have a third child, even though I had no intention of doing so. When I became pregnant, I saw it as a sign that what the Lama had said was true and that I needed to follow his instruction.

Jack was terrified of being a father. He looked at his age and the finances we had. He believed he could never afford to have a child. He said we already had two children, and that was enough. He loved them as his own. He didn't need to have a biological child to be a parent. This would be too great a burden for us financially.

We fought without mercy. The fear was overwhelming, suffocating us both. My stubbornness and devotion to the Lama, without compromise, was threatening our existence. The stress and tension, between work and my new pregnancy, were destroying my stomach. My old pattern of not making it to the bathroom had returned with a vengeance, far worse than previously. I would not relent. Jack could leave if he wanted – I was having this child.

I found a midwife. I'd had a wonderful experience delivering Indigo at home, and I was certain I could do it again, nine years later. This was all new to Jack. His friends did not have their kids at home. But with each passing month he came to trust the midwife, as she made her monthly, then weekly visits, to check on the progress of our baby. He was uncertain, and he fought to remain aloof, until his natural protective instincts overcame his doubts.

I worked as long as I could, until it became too much. My boss expected me to run, and to keep the same pace and high energy I'd had before I was pregnant. I would go almost a whole day without eating more than a protein bar, or grabbing a handful of M & M's as I raced by the front desk at the office. I couldn't keep that up.

I told her I needed to have a lunch break. I had never had a scheduled lunch or break time once in the four, almost five years I had worked for her. She said no, we didn't have time. I could carry a cooler in my car with whatever food I needed, and eat when I had a chance, which meant on the run, literally.

I began complaining to Jack that it was too much. My stomach was cramping with the stress, and I was afraid I might have a miscarriage. I quit my job, effective immediately. Jack was always supportive of me, and never wanted anyone to take advantage of me or abuse me in anyway. My boss begged me to stay, saying we could make it work, and if not, at least until I could train someone else to do what I had done. I agreed to stay until October 1, 2008. The market crashed just days after I left. By no small miracle, I avoided the chaos of that time in the real-estate market.

It took only three hours from the beginning of contractions to delivery for my son Viktor to be born, in the safety of Jack's arms, in our own bedroom. From that moment Jack's heart melted, and I knew he would give his life for his son. I was thankful we had endured our struggles, to find love waiting on the other side. The birth of our son was a beautiful blessing. Jack has thanked me many times for my stubbornness, and for my willingness to see my pregnancy through despite the fears, fighting and stress we'd endured.

Our fighting was not over, though. We had a new baby, and only one income. The stress and fighting had no chance for resolution or peace. The winds of change would not relent. We had no choice but to become stronger, greater than we had ever been before. There would be no settling, no accepting anything less than our best effort.

The stress of work, my pregnancy and our fighting had created the perfect storm for my digestive system.

I hold all my stress in my stomach. I developed food intolerances and sensitivities that left my body a wreck. My body was rotting from the inside out. I developed Leaky Gut Syndrome and an intolerance to gluten, soy and dairy.

It took me close to a year of study and research to finally self-diagnose my symptoms and find the right naturopath to help me. I found a kind young woman who offered a program of elimination, repair and reintroduction that helped me to sufficiently heal my body. I could now run errands without fear of soiling my pants or running to the bathroom four to five times before I was able to make it through the checkout line and back to the safety of my car.

I was becoming adept at handling storms. I had systems in place; I was prepared for anything. I could allow the storm to hit me full force and I would pop back up without hesitation, with no emotional reaction or response lingering within me. I was not the victim. I would tell myself, "Shit happens." It would send me into peals of laughter and giggles in the middle of a public bathroom, as it was quite literally true for me. There was nothing else to be done, no need to cry about it. It was funny to me by this point in my life. I had been through so much that this was nothing on the scale of critical events.

It was the small stuff now that stressed me out: being on time for appointments, finding my way across town to places I had never visited. The big things –

fights that threatened divorce, soiling my pants in public, separation and devastation – were nothing to me. Humiliation in front of strangers made me laugh. I was no longer capable of being embarrassed or worried about what others might think. I had sunk too low for that to be important any longer.

These events no longer aroused emotion within me. All I cared was that I was heard, that my point was made, that it was ground in to Jack's being until he surrendered. He was the only one whose opinion mattered to me – the only one I cared enough to fight with or who aroused my stubborn streak. I cared what he thought about me, and if he thought I was doing my best. In short, I loved him.

Katelyn and Mom

Katelyn repeatedly told me I should leave, get divorced. She would never tolerate or accept such behavior from a partner, spiritual teacher, boss – no one. She gave the same advice to my mom on many occasions as well. She was willing to shut people out, leave them and set absolute boundaries, enforced with an iron fist. My sister could barely speak to me, seeing what I was allowing and experiencing in my life. She simply wouldn't talk about it, if I wasn't willing to do what she thought was best.

My mom never pressured me. She struggled with a lot of the same issues in her life as I did in my own.

She and I were too willing to submit, be the good girl and not cause conflict or controversy. My mom offered support, saying I could bring the kids with me and move back to her house, leave New Mexico and all of this behind me if I needed to. She never told me what to do. She listened, and let me know that she loved me dearly and would be there for me and the kids, without question. She proved it every day in so many ways.

Jack and I fought far more violently, with scarier confrontations, than I ever had with Peter. I would call my mom, terrified of his raging emotions. He never held anything back. He would yell and scream as he struggled to communicate how he felt. The result was that it all came out as rage, far beyond frustration.

He was so frustrated that I wouldn't listen, and he couldn't articulate how he felt in words. He felt that I didn't care about how all of our struggles and financial burdens affected him. He felt that I wouldn't help him with all the responsibilities bearing down on him. He was determined to protect our family. He knew what I had experienced in my past, but he couldn't do it alone.

After every fight, Jack would take some time alone, then think and formulate the words he would use to express the essence of how he felt without rage. He would come back to me and say he was sorry for all the hurtful things he had said, and explain his point without anger or passion. He would reflect, gain a new perspective, tearfully apologize, tell me how much he loved me and say that he never wanted to live without me or the kids. He accepted that I needed to make my own decisions, even if he thought the choice was wrong or would cause us financial difficulty.

I would accept his apology and we would move forward. It took time, but eventually I learned to apologize as well. I was adamant that I would not lose my power. I didn't understand the courage it took to say you were sorry, especially when you believed you were right, for the sake of peace and for the bigger picture of keeping the family together.

As I embraced and accepted myself, I became capable of embracing and accepting others. All the fear and anxiety began to release, healing with time and wisdom. Jack and I fought every possible scenario of our fears – and we found them empty and without merit. We came to recognize when fear was ruling our thoughts, and now we no longer engage in battle to release our fears.

My cycle had kept repeating without end, without escape. I had run so many times in my life that I refused to run anymore. I was going to face this and make my relationship work. I was finally willing to fight for myself, our marriage and our family. We were worth fighting for. Jack loved us all so deeply, I am certain I will never fathom the depth of his love.

Chapter 21

Spiritual Teachers and Gurus

The only thing left standing in our way to marital bliss was my devotion to my spiritual growth. I saw it as a good and noble thing. I felt spiritually superior to Jack and would not listen to his wisdom and common sense. He couldn't understand why I was still following these spiritual teachers and giving my money and power away. He knew how strong I was with him, how I wouldn't take any crap. He couldn't understand why I couldn't see, couldn't hear the truth and stand up to these people. He knew without question that I already had all the answers I needed within me.

I had begun taking courses online with spiritual teachers, learning meditations, and studying angelology. I went to seminars and weekend retreats, meditating and walking labyrinths. If someone had a positive spiritual experience or liked a particular guru, I would follow along, paying as I went.

I even flew to Arizona to attend a weekend retreat with the Lama, despite Jack's protests. The Lama's following had increased to an international community of many devoted students. I still tried to hide my devotion to this guru from Jack. I mediated twice a day without fail, following the guidelines of his particular training. My friends only consisted of those who also followed the various teachers and gurus I followed. I couldn't yet gain awareness of my loss of power in this situation, at my own hands, by my own choice.

This was how every relationship had been for me, except for my relationship with Jack. I would devote myself completely, surrendering my voice, wisdom, decisions and power to another. I was committed to figuring out what it was within me that was allowing this, attracting this to me. I was determined to understand what I thought I was lacking, and believed I had to seek outside of myself.

The source of all of this was within me. The source of the pattern was me. I would master this pattern, learn it, understand it and thrive beyond it. I would find my own guidance; a guidance I could trust without question, with no strings or financial costs attached. I was committed to breaking free of my need for gurus and giving away my money and power.

After all I had been through, I had become the fighter. The one who wouldn't stay down, who refused to give up or surrender, despite the pleas of those who loved me. I made mistakes, got frightened by the way others behaved and treated me, and continued on. I forgave myself and kept trying. I accepted that I wasn't perfect, and that was all right.

I stopped feeling pity for myself, believing myself to be the victim. I knew who I was, and I continued to move forward into the light each day as best I could. It took years for me to understand that my relationships were a reflection of my own thoughts, fears and projections, that I didn't trust others because I didn't trust myself to make the right choices. As I gained this understanding, the obstacles and hindrances I placed upon myself began to fall away. I accepted responsibility as the creator of my life.

With that wisdom, I burned all of the physical objects I had held onto, the things I believed to be sacred gifts that were required for me to attain enlightenment. I burned away the power they held over me. Through the flames and smoke of acceptance, I released the power I had given away. I freed my will and my power to return to me.

From the ashes I rose again, new, clean and transformed. I cleansed my thoughts of the programming I had received. I turned to my husband, held him tightly, thanked him for his strength, endurance and fortitude. He had never given up, never abandoned me when I needed him most. I stepped forward and felt what it was like to make my own decisions without influence from gurus and spiritual teachers.

Honestly, I was not able to recognize my pattern with spiritual teachers and gurus until I began writing this book. I could not see that Jack had been right all along. I couldn't admit that I was giving away my power and my money in hopes of receiving the blessing of being a good and obedient girl. I couldn't accept that I had been placing my intent upon the reward of enlightenment to affirm that I was worthy of existing. I wasn't willing to believe that I was valuable, just as I am. I had to be special in some way to receive love. In recognizing my patterns and being willing to share them, I was able to focus my attention on the big picture.

I was able to see and understand the intentions and motivations of those who have played a part in my life, as they became clear in this writing. Once and for all I was able to acknowledge Jack's role in my life as protector, not one who had any intention to cause me harm. All he had ever wanted was to protect me and make me happy. Regardless of this new awareness, I acknowledge that my past perceptions of Jack were what I was capable of understanding at the time. I forgive myself for the time it has taken me to arrive at this moment. I couldn't have done it any sooner than right now.

Jack has forgiven me each time I denied him – while I was seeking instead the love and approval of a spiritual teacher or guru over him – and for the toll it has taken on our family. When I finally stood before him and told him that he was right all along and that I was sorry, it nearly killed him. In fact, he was indignant that I would even acknowledge his part at all, as it was so late in coming. He grabbed the calculator and tallied the total; it had taken me four thousand, three hundred days of fighting and conflict with him for me to finally admit that he was right. I had to laugh, when I finally conceded; I gave in and admitted he was right – and that's when he got mad and lost patience with me. It was as if the act of surrender itself, on my part, was enough to push him over the edge.

Act 5

Chapter 22
Origin of Pattern

There was no mirror to reflect back at me, as I stood in the far back section of the yard at my childhood home. I couldn't look myself in the eyes and tell myself lies, force myself to believe I was worthless, without value or purpose. Awareness was fighting its way to the surface of my being, shattering this long-held illusion.

I had eaten a big piece of angel-food cake smothered in strawberries, mashed into a sauce and sweetened with sugar. A dollop of homemade whipped cream graced the top. It was my younger brother's favorite birthday cake. It was his seventh birthday and we were celebrating his special day. I was fifteen years old, eight years his senior.

I ate the cake with delight, devouring it in a few large gulps. I was starving, having not eaten all day. The sugar raced into my bloodstream. I could feel the renewed energy revive my exhausted body. The guilt flushed my face with shame, red as the strawberries. What had I done? I had lost all self-control. I had promised myself I wouldn't touch a bite of the birthday cake. There were way too many calories in that for me to touch it.

I had failed; I was a loser who had no control over myself. I hated myself for this weakness. Now I was going to be fat. My legs would never look as skinny as they had in my childhood photo that I kept in my room to remind me of my goal. I was to be as thin as I was when I was eight years old. I loved how I looked in that photo. I was happy, smiling. My legs were thin and beautiful, and I was free.

The guilt and shame washed over me, as sticky as black tar. I was fat, dumb and weak. The emotions were so great that I had to release them, purge them from my body. I had to regain control and punish my weakness. I couldn't be fat; the shame and embarrassment of being fat were far greater than any fear I had of being caught throwing up, purging my body, by the guests at my brother's party.

I walked quietly to the backyard, knowing soon I would be free of the calories I had consumed. My weakness expelled from my body. I allowed the cruel voice and thoughts to take over until it all came thrusting out of my mouth, as my body lurched forward. Bending deeply, I got as close to the earth as I could to release the vomit, as far away from my clothes and shoes as possible.

The bright red of the freshly eaten strawberries showed brightly, clashing against the fresh-cut green grass. I was standing with only the apple tree to support me. The purple crocuses and yellow daffodils were my witnesses. Somehow it all seemed so wrong this time. I could see my situation for the ugliness it was.

The grass was living and full of color. I leaned forward, my hand pressed into the bark of the tree. Weakened by a lack of calories and self-abuse, the skin of my hand looked sallow and dull. I could see the blue of my veins through the thin skin, delicately covering my arms. My long hair had lost its luster, made brittle and breaking, as I held it away from my face to vomit. I looked down at my body and wondered why I was so angry with my appearance, and the perceived weakness of feeding myself, or actually enjoying my brother's birthday cake.

I felt ridiculous sneaking outside to throw up, with the house full of people, while I was hiding outside. I stood upright and said out loud, "That's it. I'm done, this is stupid." The living color of nature surrounded me with the shelter of its silence as it pressed awareness into my vision and my mind. The mirror gone, I couldn't feed myself the required dose of self-hate to seal the pattern in place. I couldn't stand before my own image, look into my own eyes and witness the suffering and pain scarred into my face. Without that image, I couldn't curse my very existence. All I could see was the beauty of nature, the vibrancy of the colors that surrounded me. All I could hear were the cries of the birds sounding alarms at my gurgled purging.

My whole family knew I had an eating disorder. They would laugh at me at dinner, saying, "Why give any to her? She's just going to throw it up anyway." I would hear, "Do the dishes after you throw up," as I went into the bathroom to unleash my self-abuse. Sometimes they would make comments about my weight, and that I was getting too skinny – but mostly it was not addressed, brushed under the table. Most people simply didn't know what to say. They used abusive and confrontational language in hopes that I might snap out of it, but it never worked. That was the same language I used with myself. What I needed, what I was desperately seeking, was love – the acceptance of who I was without reservation or excuse.

I continued to struggle with body issues and acceptance for years. The abuse had stopped – self-care and nurturing took its place – but that voice could still find a way of getting into my ear. I greeted it with kindness as often as I could. I would find something flattering to wear or say about myself. I make healthy choices now, I exercise, and I focus on allowing acceptance to wash over me. With time and perseverance, the voice has lost its power.

Reflections

As I sip my homemade green smoothie from a tall, round glass, I reflect back to the beginning of my self-abuse and lack of self-esteem. I think about the time I first struggled with power, with the need to control what I ate and decide for myself what was best. I was two years old. It was evening and I was at my grandparents' house, sitting in the same wooden highchair my mother had sat in before me.

I can remember every detail. Where the chair was placed, at the edge of the kitchen, where I could clearly see what my grandpa was making for me to eat. Only the light over the stove and a small light over the kitchen table were turned on. The large picture window darkened the kitchen.

My grandpa was making oatmeal with raisins for me to eat for dinner. I didn't like raisins. I told my grandpa I didn't want raisins. He said, "Whaaat? What do you mean you don't like raisins? I'm having raisins in my oatmeal. You're going to eat the oatmeal with raisins, now that's enough." I said, "No. No, I'm not eating raisins. I don't want them. Take them out."

Grandpa cried out to God, praying as he kneeled beside my highchair with his hand upon my head, "Please, God, do not allow her to be a stubborn and obstinate child. Break her will, that she will learn to submit to you." I had to sit in that highchair, in the darkened kitchen, for hours by myself, because I wouldn't eat the raisins he put in my oatmeal.

I wasn't a good girl because I didn't like raisins the way grandpa did. My voice, my choice, my exerting control and power over my own life was not acceptable. God would break me so that I would learn to submit. I was bad, and I was going to hell if I didn't obey and eat those God damn raisins.

I didn't eat those raisins that day. I said no. I stood in my power, made my choice and spoke my truth. My will grew strong within me. I stayed in that chair until my father sneaked in and stole me away. He had suffered under the domination of two alcoholics and knew my pain. It wasn't until I'd begun writing this book that I learned that my mother was sobbing in the other room, wanting desperately to intervene, but her father commanded her to stay out of it. My father, on the other hand, had authority as the head of the household. He was given the power to intervene, to stand between my grandpa and me. When he couldn't stand the abuse any further, he freed me from my grandpa and that highchair.

I may have won that battle, as I was freed without eating the raisins, but my grandpa succeeded in breaking my spirit that day. The lesson he wanted me to learn seeped deep within my psyche, hidden away from conscious thought and awareness for years to come. It influenced my confidence; my sense of self-worth, value and esteem. I became fearful of speaking up, making choices, being anything but the good and obedient girl I was expected to be. All I wanted was to be loved and accepted, to seek approval and do God's will, so that grandpa would love me.

My eating disorder began when I was twelve years old. I used my strength, the years of internal messaging that said I wasn't good enough. I used my own inner voice to bully myself into believing I was undeserving of love and acceptance. That voice was cruel, hateful and powerful.

I made myself believe I was unworthy and undeserving of receiving anything but abuse. I projected this belief outward as an inability to enjoy and receive food. My inner voice telling me, "You are fat, dumb and ugly," developed into an eating disorder to cope with the abuse. The belief of my mind transmuted into physical torment.

I recounted everything that made me feel unworthy in my own mind. My nervous cough would kick in and I would throw it all up. I would throw up all the words, the beliefs and feelings that hurt me. My pattern of abuse and release began, the core of my pattern being a lack of self-esteem and confidence in my own worth as a human being deserving of love.

I can remember the first time I threw up as if it were yesterday. I had eaten a chocolate-chip cookie with extra-large chocolate chips, sneaking it from the kitchen when no one was looking. I ate it joyfully in the corner of the kitchen, facing out the window to the backyard. I immediately felt guilt.

I went to an old closet that had been converted into a makeshift powder room, looked in the mirror and told myself, "You have no self-control. You are weak, fat and ugly." I threw it up, got it out of me. I took back my self-control, my power, by throwing up what I had done in weakness. My abuse was my strength in my twisted beliefs. I could remove any mistakes I made by controlling, limiting what I could receive, and removing anything I saw as weakness.

I laughed out loud, realizing that throwing up was the perfect solution to my dilemma of guilt, judgment and weakness. Proud of finding a way to enjoy food and still maintain my faulty beliefs, I hollered up the stairs to my sister to share my revelation. She responded, "You're a dumbass." My belief was cemented; I was undeterred. I knew I had found a way to have fun, appear to engage in life and still give that voice authority over me, through self-abuse.

One winter day I was walking home from school, instead of taking the bus, when I began to black out. The lack of nutrients and years of abuse was wearing on my body's ability to survive. I desperately needed nourishment. I was too weak to walk home.

A neighborhood boy had been walking with me to keep me safe, and seeing I was near collapse, he lay face down in the snow and had me sit on his back until I was steady enough to continue. I can remember my gratitude and embarrassment at his willingness to risk his own well-being to keep me from harm. If only I had been half as willing as he was to protect myself, how different things would have been.

I was five foot eight inches, averaging 100 to 105 pounds. I can remember a day when I couldn't stop bleeding from my nose. It lasted all day, becoming a fusion of blood and water. I was leaking my internal fluids from my nostrils, barely maintaining consciousness. The solution? My dad bought me vitamins, the symptoms went away, and the bleeding stopped. I was cured.

My belief system was never questioned by my family; my self-abuse never addressed. No questions were ever asked as to why I was doing this. The immediate crisis was averted; that was all that was required. If the problem wasn't acknowledged it didn't exist – no one was to blame and nothing had to be changed.

My wake-up call was not to come for another year, by a shift in my own awareness. It ended as quickly and seamlessly as it began, throwing up in the backyard during my brother's birthday party. This was the first time I threw up outside. It made all the difference. Nature could show me what my own reflection never could. I was fifteen years old when awareness grabbed hold and held me in silence.

Chapter 23

Root Cause

With my chair pulled close to the window, the light surrounding me in warmth and my plants filling the room to overflowing, I stop and consider my pattern. I recognize my life lesson and I accept it. I breathe it in to my heart and release all blame, forgiving myself and others. I glance at the snow-covered mountain before me – steadfast and unmoving, yet ever changing, cycling with the seasons – and I thank those who have been in my life to help me learn.

I have created these experiences to understand, to become who I was meant to become. Like the mountain I am steadfast, and in constant evolution. I created the environment to be controlled; I allowed myself to be manipulated in relationships. I abused myself, giving up my power, giving up my voice, being the victim, getting lost in the dreams of someone else. I let my energy be corded and pulled in a thousand disparate directions.

I waited until I was pushed far enough, the storm sharp enough, that I could hear, see and change. Only then did I stand up and say, "I have the power within me at all times – it is an illusion that I do not have access to unlimited power." I can only be a victim when I do not take responsibility for my choices and actions, and in so doing, I take back my power. I have not had these experiences because I am weak or deserving of such abuse – I have had them to learn, understand and grow stronger.

I have found myself through acceptance in this moment. My self-esteem has not always been the best; I accept that. I forgive myself for all that I believed was true and limiting. I forgive myself for not loving myself, for not believing I was worthy of being protected or receiving love. I forgive myself for not allowing myself to have my own dream, to fulfill the desires of my heart and the purpose of my soul.

In this moment, as I reflect back – sitting in the sunlight, in the safety of my own home – I catch myself trying to edit my story, my experiences, based on who I am now and who I think might be listening to my words, these thoughts revealed on paper. Will they still accept me if they know my story, if I hold nothing back? I speak in pieces, weakly tied together, allowing listeners to pick up what they will; to find what seeds remain, what is left unspoken.

I struggle, knowing that I must first accept myself so that others may accept me fully. I must stop trying to edit out my mistakes, my judgments of self and others, and allow it all to open – to unfold before me on these pages, and in my life. If I am to be of service to anyone, I must first be of service to myself. I must heal these wounds – find what outdated beliefs still linger in the recesses of my mind – and release them back into the light.

I have been a victim by my own choice. I have tried to be the good girl, not allowing myself to be fully engaged, expressed wholly as I am. The good girl can't accept that she has done wrong, isn't right or could have intentionally caused harm. The good girl loves – and does not place walls of ice to separate herself from everyone else.

The good girl forgives, and she makes excuses to protect those who have hurt her. She doesn't hold herself or others accountable for their actions. The good girl doesn't become angry, fierce, loud or outspoken. I am not – and do not need to be – a good girl any longer. I do not have to edit myself so that others may like and accept me.

All that matters is that I like and accept myself; that I am connected with the wisdom and guidance of my own heart. I am all aspects of life, I express all emotions, I am all actions – all choices – both good and evil. I am sick and tired of trying to be the good girl. I am exhausted and bored with trying. I will be me without excuses, without reasons to justify my choices and behavior.

I seek the wisdom and counsel of my heart, and I follow it whether or not its guidance is easy or acceptable to others. Their acceptance is of no matter, and the difficulty has no bearing. I will evolve at my own pace, in my own direction, in perfect time. I will follow the wisdom held within the peace and beauty of my heart.

When I first looked back and reflected upon my experiences and patterns, I believed that I had not been truly triumphant, and that my current marriage was not something I or others could view as a success. My triumph didn't look the way I thought it would. My perfect marriage was not like the pictures or romantic movies. It didn't follow the parameters of acceptable behavior. It's loud, raucous and fierce. Yet it *is* absolutely perfect, just as it is. My husband is and was exactly what I needed him to be through it all.

I had shut others out, for fear they couldn't accept a marriage as raw and honest as mine has been. From the outside it may have appeared abusive, cruel and out of control. That has never been the case. My marriage to Jack is gentle and forgiving. It allows the self and the other to fall short, fail, learn, get angry, say hurtful things and have love and forgiveness endure through it all. It is a marriage that expresses it all, every color of emotion. I have been the victim and the enemy of myself and of my husband. I have also been the lover, the friend and the holder of all that is honest, loyal and true.

The Gift

Without my husband Jack, I could never have survived the years of manipulation and control that I experienced at the hand of so-called gurus and spiritual teachers. I fought with and questioned my husband, looking down on his spiritual wisdom, as he saw through the guises of the gurus and their self-created systems. He warned me, as we argued, not to give these people any money. He told me I didn't need them, or their practices and meditations, to have a direct connection with God. His sole intention was to protect me with every ounce of his being.

Out of guilt and desperation I would hide my expenditures, the true cost of my studies and practices, from Jack's prying eyes. I would hand over my money time and again to others, receiving no lasting or tangible results for my fervor. I forgive myself for this part of my journey, my pattern of self-destruction. I forgive those I so willing gave my power to, and I ask Jack to forgive me for the worry without end that he endured for my safety.

I wanted to stop repeating my pattern of getting lost, of giving up my power, but I couldn't. I continued being incapable of maintaining a sense of self, separate and distinct from others, including false gurus and spiritual teachers. Jack stood as my witness through it all, hand outstretched, if only I was willing to take it.

My beliefs have changed with the wind, evolved with the storms. I have released a relentless torrent of emotions and expression through this journey of transformation. I have come to understand that I am the ever-present witness to my becoming. I am everything and nothing. I am unlimited potential and possibility, in the process of becoming fully expressed without limit. I am separate and distinct, and a part of the whole of all life.

My logical, safe and steady husband has stood firm, rooted deeply in his commitment to me, our marriage and our family. I am forever grateful for his strength, courage and compassionate heart. He was always there for me, telling me I could quit, that I didn't have to take the abuse, or work for cruel and demanding bosses. He would take care of me, protect me. He was strong enough to carry the brunt of the load. That is exactly what he has done, waiting patiently for me to become who I was meant to be. He has only ever wanted my happiness.

The irony is that now that I see and thank him for his enduring love, he can't take it. It has become the straw that breaks the camel's back. The acknowledgment of his struggle makes the pain, heartache and years of conflict too great to bear in his memory. I hold him now as he releases the burden of protecting me, knowing that he has succeeded. I am safe, I love him, the battle he has fought at my side has been won. He, too, is freed by my willingness to stand up and be me.

The truth is that there is nothing to edit, nothing to hide in my story. There is no predetermined message that is of more value than what I have learned through my own direct experience. Life is not about comparing my story to the story of others. It's about living, accepting, allowing, and transitioning to a new level of being. It's not about getting shattered once, being broken by life's experiences one time and then it will never happen again. I didn't become empowered once and never give my power away from that day forward. Life is about being willing to continually be in process, shattering into being, to reveal the beacon of light within.

Chapter 24

Shattered Into Being

As I reflect back, I have come to understand my experience of breaking. It is like a storm that overwhelms my senses. I deny myself the love I need to survive – I refuse to forgive my weakness and I cry out. I ask for what I cannot give, and in its place I punish myself for my lack of self-esteem and confidence.

In that moment – at my lowest point, believing myself not worthy to live – I cry out and beg to be released from this life, to be freed from this body. I feel the abandonment as I separate from myself, denying myself the love that I seek. My emotions rage within me, as I wish beyond hope or reason that I might find kindness in the hearts of others as I desperately seek acceptance outside of myself. I break, cry out, and beg for mercy; for the light to flood over me and wash away my pain.

That is why the mirror has been so instrumental in my self-messaging and programming; I look into my own eyes as I cry out. I am crying out to me, to rescue myself. After I have broken, after I have cried all the tears I have to give, I look into my own eyes again – I pause and observe my face as a stranger, and I finally see what is really present. I take notice of the mascara blackening my face in streaks running down my cheeks, my eyes bloodied and made red by my tears. In that instant, without warning, it happens. My heart breaks for the suffering and pain I have experienced. I see the child staring back at me. I feel compassion, bubbling from within. The dam I have created breaks forth, and all I have ever wanted, ever needed, rushes to me. That child within reaches her small hand to me. I grasp hold, pulling toward her, and I receive the love, warmth and acceptance I have been seeking with all my being.

The time has come for me to forgive myself, to wrap my arms around myself, and say, "You are going to be all right. I love you. You are beautiful, you are a beacon of light in the darkness, shattering into being. Do not forget who you are and where you are going. Your suffering has not been in vain. It has been a gift, a blessing on your journey back home, to the wisdom of your heart."

I am and have always been worthy. I have been present this whole time. I hid, acted weak, played the victim – experiencing this dense, material life and feeling all it had to offer – being afraid of who I truly am, my power within. I sought guidance, wisdom, direction outside of myself, through meditation,

Eastern practices, angel teachings; anything I could find that might give me a glimmer of peace or hope.

I rise up now and lay my hand upon my heart and breathe. I go deep within, eyes closed, and allow myself to feel the warm touch of the sun upon my skin. The healing begins. I absorb the wisdom, strength and grounding coming from deep within the Earth. I know I cannot lose who I am. I cannot separate from my true self.

I cannot fall short or make a mistake that is not a critical part of my growth in this life. I am learning without end, following love back home, never giving up. I surrender all but my will and intention to find my way. I remember the power I hold within, held safe, at peace in my heart. I can never truly be lost, broken or separated. It is all an illusion – and I release it.

I no longer place hope outside of myself, in the hands of others. I am the watcher, the observer of life without judgment. I release all the fears that made me a nervous wreck, running to the bathroom. I shield and protect myself, while allowing myself to get lost, shattered and broken. This is how I have become stronger, more complete – through breaking.

Being broken, and sobbing on the floor, is the most beautiful gift I have been given upon this Earth. In that moment on the razor's edge, when I finally slip over the cliff onto the rocks below, I surrender. I no longer exist, I can no longer try. I am torn apart, weak, broken, utterly without hope. Fear of death has no hold on my heart. It is in that exact moment when I begin again. I reach for my heart. I am alive, allowing the transformation to happen. I understand what it is to be human. I embrace the full, direct experience of the illusion of separation – and I know it to be false.

When I become challenged, I find new ways to empower change through clear action. I surrender to the fact that if it is happening, it is exactly what should be happening. It is the exact experience needed to release old beliefs, thoughts, ideas or actions – and move forward.

I must feel this experience directly, and know it to be true; feeling it on a cellular level creates true and lasting change. This is what it means for me to become empowered, to be in a place where I can set a new course, create a life of value and purpose. I accept what is happening, allowing the response to rise from within my heart – to be in a place of knowing, accepting that the response given is always perfect. There is no wrong answer, no wrong choice. Each choice leads me further down the path to wisdom, understanding and experience. For my beliefs to change I must be challenged by the storms of life.

Cycles continue, and that is not wrong. I become confused – I lose clarity – it is all perfect. I question, observe, reaching for the child within. I am gentle with myself, held in the heart of peace. I know how to find my way out. I become aware and become my own witness, observing my responses and the words and actions I take.

I was gifted with an access code, a heart-wisdom tool when I needed it most, through a book written by David McArthur, *Your Spiritual Heart*. This book confirmed what I knew to be true all along. It reminded me to trust myself to follow the steps necessary to access my heart's wisdom whenever I need it.

The steps given in this book are simple and profound. From awareness, I reach out and touch my heart, breathing through it. I experience the memory of love, of joy, of gratitude and appreciation. I radiate within, with all the aspects of love. I ask myself the question, and I am guided by the wisdom heart, my true self, my spiritual self. I am guided by the most deeply held values of my soul.

I have struggled, not trusting myself, seeking guidance only to find silence or those who would take advantage of me when I needed love the most. I sought to fulfill the deepest desires of my heart, and I gave away my power for a false promise. The spiritual wisdom of my heart was always there, waiting for me to listen and follow – my own guiding tool within.

I have found my pattern, the root cause of my experience of pain and suffering. There is no wrong turn, no mistake – it is all learning. I accept that challenge and frustration are necessary for change;

transforming me to greater acceptance, knowing and wisdom.

The storms of life bring me back to the wisdom of my heart. Confusion brings about the questions needed. Once I have connected to my heart, I am brought to a place of clarity, where the most effective actions are revealed. I am filled with peace, resolute in my confidence of what needs to be.

There is nothing left to do but stand, hold my ground and be firm. I am free, deserving of love, and open to receive and to give. I am a part of all that is. I am a part of the suffering of all humanity. I am a part of the joyous celebration of all life. I watch it flow around and through me. I feel it – like the warm sun upon my skin – the gentle breeze of summer.

Nothing matters; life is fine, no matter what happens. I can always find my way back home, deep within my soul. I am my own security, my own safety. I can never lose who I am. I can never be dissolved to nothing, no matter how hard I try. I am whole, at peace, complete – just as I am. No more worries about being controlled or manipulated. I forgive myself for it all. I forgive those who taught me what I needed to understand. It has led me to this moment. I am alive with unconditional love and compassion.

We each have our own message, our own patterns, beliefs and core values in this life. I now know that no matter how many times I get lost, angry or frustrated –

fall short of my truth or give away my power – I can always find my way back to who I am. All the experiences and lessons I have endured have been necessary, forcing me to trust myself. They have made me the person I am today. They have allowed me to continue shattering into being, becoming the beacon of light that I am, until I am without limit, living in the light of the sun. They have reminded me that I can always connect to and hear the wisdom of my heart, that I have within me all the guidance I will ever need – an internal compass, a North Star – that seeks only the highest and best for myself and for all living beings.

I never have to seek to be loved, accepted, guided or protected, outside of what I can directly experience from within my own heart. I do not have to give away my power to receive. I do not have to pay to receive guidance or love. The Divine Love and Spiritual Guidance I seek with all of my heart is ever present. I only need to become aware, reach for the beating rhythm of my being. My own heart is the source of all guidance.

I do not have to be liked and accepted by all. I can make enemies, release relationships, cause frustration for myself and others, and still be Divinely guided by the wisdom of my own heart. I am allowed to be all aspects of my becoming without judgment of myself. I am allowed to be strong, to be a beacon of light, without guilt or shame. I am allowed to have abundance, to receive all that life has to offer. I am allowed to have peace and eternal joy. I am allowed to Be Love – to feel it, experience it – in every cell of my being. I am the warmth, love and acceptance I seek – and I remember this truth when I need it most.

Glinda, the good witch in the Wizard of Oz, said to Dorothy in the end, "You've always had the power, my dear; you just had to learn it for yourself." That is the summation of my life. I have had the power within me all along; all the lessons and life experiences that I've faced were what I needed to shatter the shell that held the great light and truth that I am within. I am a beacon shattering into being, following the wisdom of my heart to greater awareness and wholeness each day.

"What I am looking for is not out there, it is in me."

Helen Keller

Invocation

I have Shattered Into Being and I continue, as a beacon, shattering into being every day.

My hope and prayer is that you too will find your way to shatter, releasing what has been, and allowing your own inner wisdom to guide you on your path toward fully becoming who you were meant to be. Many blessings to you always, as you journey through time and space within the vast expanse of your own heart. May you find your way deep within the Light, back to the Source of All Life, enveloped in everlasting LOVE.

About the Author

I, Anastacia Jayet, am not simply my name. I identified by six legal names by the time I was thirty-one years old. I am not my title, my job or the place where I live. I have had many titles, experienced many diverse jobs and moved many times. I lived many years adrift without knowing who I was. I lacked self-esteem and confidence, disconnected from all that surrounded me. I journeyed, studied and experienced many concepts of myself through many different lenses of perception – until I realized that I am unlimited, ever changing yet constant – and that everything is possible and a potential part of my becoming. I am at peace in the eye of the storm. That is who I am. I have learned to accept all aspects of myself by surrendering, trusting, allowing, receiving and accepting all that is.

Book Summary

This poignant story tells of personal tragedy and triumph, of getting lost and finding the internal compass – one's own North Star – to take responsibility for creating a life of value and purpose. It acknowledges that a lack of self-esteem and confidence is at the root of victimization – that taking responsibility for personal choice and action brings empowerment – and that forgiving oneself, while releasing blame, removes the final obstacles to freedom and eternal joy.

Target Audience

Readers of *Shattered Into Being* are seeking to regain their personal power; to strengthen their self-esteem and confidence. They have survived personal tragedy and are inspired to find and recognize their own life pattern. They have a desire to be empowered – to use the wisdom of their heart and their own experiences – to live life on purpose.

Format

Short, quick, inspirational

Contact and Engagements

Please contact Anastacia Jayet for Speaking Engagements, Workshops, Seminars and Interviews through:

MANNARA LLC
A BEACON SHATTERING INTO BEING

223 N Guadalupe #296
Santa Fe, NM 87501
MANNARALLC.com
Anastacia@AnastaciaJayet.com

For Blogs, offering additional insights into my experiences, please visit my website at AnastaciaJayet.com

Please sign up for my free Newsletter at AnastaciaJayet.com

If you would like to contact me, or would like more information about my book, please write to:
MANNARA LLC
Attention: Anastacia Jayet
223 N Guadalupe #296
Santa Fe, NM 87501

Or via email at:
Anastacia@AnastaciaJayet.com

"Lighthouses don't go running all over an island looking for boats to save; they just stand there shining."

Anne Lamott